DELIVER US

TRUE STORIES OF POSSESSION, OPPRESSION AND SPIRITUAL WARFARE

MARY ROMASANTA

Sagga Publishing House LLC

SAGGA PUBLISHING HOUSE LLC, February 2026

Copyright © 2026 by Mary Romasanta

Premium Mass-Market Hardback ISBN: 978-1-964642-30-7

Premium Mass-Market Paperback ISBN: 978-1-964642-29-1

eBook ISBN: 978-1-964642-32-1

Library of Congress Control Number: 2025911388

Second edition.

This book discusses spiritual experiences and beliefs as understood by the author. Readers are encouraged to use personal discernment and seek appropriate professional or pastoral guidance where necessary.

Published in the United States by Sagga Publishing House LLC, San Antonio, Texas.

Visit the author's website at www.maryromasanta.com

Printed in the United States of America

ALSO BY MARY ROMASANTA:

Avici Sagga
The Eternal Secret
Infestation
Oscar
La Llorona: The Awakening

For previews of upcoming books and information about the author, visit
www.saggapublishing.com.
Follow the author on Instagram @AuthorMaryRomasanta.

This book is dedicated to my husband, Robert, who walks beside me in faith, who sees both the beauty and the battle, and who reminds me, every single day, that faith, love, and courage were always meant to walk hand in hand.

DELIVER US

TRUE STORIES OF POSSESSION, OPPRESSION AND SPIRITUAL WARFARE

Contents

Introduction   XVII

1. The Young   3

2. The Vulnerable   15

3. The Doubted   23

4. The Intruders   29

5. The Devil's Foothold   37

6. The Summoned   47

7. The Targeted   55

8. The Shunned   61

10. The Dead Part I   83

11. The Grieving   93

12. The Lost   101

13. The Burdened   107

14. The Cursed   115

15. The Possessed   125

16. The Delivered   133

17. Conclusion   141

Afterword   145

Acknowledgements   147

More from the Author   149

About the Author   151

Deliverance (noun): The action of being rescued or liberated; freedom from bondage, danger, or suffering.

DELIVER US

US

TRUE STORIES OF
POSSESSION, OPPRESSION
AND SPIRITUAL WARFARE

Introduction

I am the daughter of a pastor and a florist—rooted in faith, grounded in beauty. A wife anchored in steadfast love. A mother, both softened and sharpened by three growing hearts. A technologist, forged in the fires of logic and precision. I am a writer gathering each of these identities, weaving them into every story I tell.

So, what qualifies me to write a nonfiction book on spiritual warfare?

I was raised in both the light of the sanctuary and the shadows that it sometimes couldn't reach. I grew up learning to discern not just right from wrong, but light from counterfeit light—to spot the difference between woundedness and wickedness, between silence and surrender.

I learned that spiritual warfare isn't a metaphor—it's a war. And the battlefield isn't always visible. It's in the mind, in the home, and in the soul.

Much of what the world dismisses as myth, fantasy, or folklore often has roots far older and deeper than we care to admit. Beneath the skepticism, beneath the noise of modern intellect and cultural detachment, lies something eternal—something that still speaks.

I was raised in a home where faith wasn't just spoken—it was lived. My childhood was spent on the front lines of prayer meetings, revivals, and deliverance sessions. I've witnessed firsthand what it means to war in the spirit, to intercede for the tormented, to discern the unseen. My father, a seasoned pastor and spiritual leader, often included me in spaces most children are shielded from.

I didn't just hear about demons and strongholds—I saw their effects. I felt their presence. I learned early that the spiritual realm is real, active, and far more personal than many are willing to believe.

In Christian theology and spiritual practice, spiritual warfare refers to the ongoing battle between the forces of God (light) and the powers of Satan (darkness). The idea that those who walk in the light of Christ are specifically targeted shows up repeatedly in Scripture, tradition, and testimony.

Like most, I've been targeted—in my work, as a wife, daughter, mother, and friend. I spent decades building a career in technology, a world grounded in systems, logic, and problem-solving. Yet even there, amid algorithms and precision, I never lost sight of the supernatural. If anything, it sharpened my discernment. It taught me to question what I see, to probe what lingers beneath the surface, and to pursue truth with both spirit and mind.

During a recent television interview with the Archdiocese of San Antonio, the reporter leaned in and asked with sincere curiosity: "Given your upbringing in the Church—and living across from a cemetery—did you have a lot of nightmares growing up?"

My answer came without hesitation: "All the time."

But they weren't just childhood nightmares—the kind that vanish with the morning sun. These dreams were vivid. Persistent. Far more terrifying than anything I've seen in horror films or even in waking life.

Growing up as a pastor's daughter in a spiritually charged environment meant I lived in a world most children are mercifully spared from. I witnessed manifestations. I saw spiritual attacks. I experienced moments that branded themselves into my memory not because of how surreal they were, but because of how real they felt.

These weren't stories told from a pulpit. They weren't metaphors. They followed me home and into my sleep. I dreamed of death long before I understood what it truly meant.

Long before I had language for loss or grief, it visited me—uninvited, unrelenting. Some nights, the dreams were painfully specific: I stood at a coffin, staring into the still face of my father or brother. The air in those funeral homes was always thick with silence, heavy with sorrow. And the ache didn't fade when I opened my eyes. It clung to me.

Other nights were darker still. Shadows with intelligence and purpose moved through my dreams. Their forms twisted with rage and something far older than fear. I witnessed demonic possessions—so violent they fractured the rules of logic. I sensed presences I couldn't see, entities that watched from behind the veil.

I'd wake up drenched in sweat, lungs heaving, heart racing, with the terrible certainty that I hadn't just been dreaming—I'd been surviving. In those moments, the line between the spiritual and the physical felt terrifyingly thin. As a child, I didn't know why the dreams came. I didn't understand what they meant. I only knew one thing: they were real. And they knew I could see them.

My writing is shaped by my journey—a life marked by faith, resilience, and a deep sensitivity to what lies hidden. Yes, I write fiction—but never for spectacle.

My stories live in the spaces between genres, where psychological thrillers collide with spiritual truths, where science fiction weaves into the supernatural. They often brush against the edges of horror, not to shock, but to *reveal*. To drag darkness into the open and examine it beneath the glare of truth. Because the battle between good and evil isn't just a metaphor. It isn't confined to pulpits or theology textbooks.

It's real. It's spiritual. It's happening all around us—inside our homes, deep within our thoughts, in the fragile spaces of our marriages and relationships. It doesn't announce itself. It creeps in, silent and patient, settling into the quiet corners of our lives where shadows grow unchecked. There, evil takes root, and doubt, fear, and anxiety whisper their poison until we can no longer tell truth from lie.

This is not a book of ghost stories.

It's not here to spook you or entertain your curiosity about the paranormal. It is not written to provoke or sensationalize. This book is a testimony—a bearing witness. A reckoning with what many would rather dismiss or forget. And more than anything, it is a declaration of the One power greater than all that haunts us. That's why I write. Not to terrify. Not to mystify. But to tell the truth.

Because evil is real—but so is deliverance. So is healing. So is victory. And sometimes, stepping into that victory requires returning to the places that once paralyzed us—not to relive the pain, but to reclaim those spaces with truth. To expose what lurks in the shadows. And to declare, with unshakable faith, that it does not win.

This book is divided into five parts, each exposing truths woven into my novels *Infestation, Oscar, The Eternal Secret, La Llorona: The Awakening* and *Avīci Sagga*.

Though fictional in structure, some of the stories within my novels are rooted in real encounters—personal experiences, generational memories, and spiritual truths I've come to know through both suffering and grace. These are not just tales born from imagination; they are shaped by the unseen forces that have stirred my life, my faith, and my calling as a writer.

The known facts of these accounts serve as a foundation—threads I've carefully gathered and woven into a greater tapestry. Some details have been lost to time, to silence, to the fragility of memory. In those moments, I've reimagined—not to distort the truth, but to honor it. Each reconstructed scene is a work of care, designed to capture the emotional and spiritual resonance of those who lived through it, often without the language to explain what they experienced.

What I've done here is not invention. It's *restoration*. Because truth doesn't always live in a flawless record or a neatly documented past. Sometimes, it pulses through what was felt—in the fear that gripped the chest like a vise, in the desperate prayers whispered through clenched teeth, in the heavy silence of a room that felt *watched*. In the presence you couldn't see, but couldn't deny. Some truths do not ask for your belief. They stand, unshaken, whether you accept them or not.

What you're about to read may unsettle you. It may sound impossible. That's all right. I'm not here to convince you. I'm here to bear witness—to the things my eyes have seen, my hands have touched, and my spirit has wrestled with in the dead of night.

This is a journey into the shadows—into the quiet places where evil waits, and into the moments when light shatters its hold. It is faith tested in fire, forged in battle, and crowned in deliverance.

Step carefully. Read with an open mind and a prayer on your lips.

-Mary Romasanta

DELIVER US

US

TRUE STORIES OF
POSSESSION, OPPRESSION
AND SPIRITUAL WARFARE

PART I

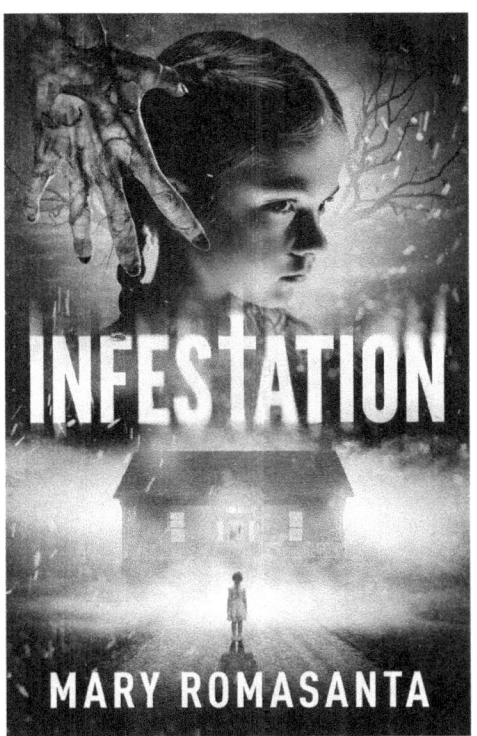

A young pastor, determined to save his failing church, moves his family into a decaying house across from a cemetery—unwittingly stepping into the grip of a malevolent force rooted in dark secrets and ancient curses. As shadows close in, only his six-year-old daughter, Emma, can see the truth—and unearth the horror waiting within.

Chapter 1

The Young

Infestation is not simply a work of fiction. It is rooted in personal accounts of events that began shortly after my parents purchased a house across from San Fernando Cemetery #2—the largest cemetery in San Antonio, Texas—and converted it into a family flower shop.

Death was no longer something we drove past. It was outside our windows. Funeral processions rolled by daily. Fresh graves marked time more reliably than holidays. Grief was constant—seasonal, visible, inescapable.

Not long after establishing the business, the woman who lived in the house directly behind the shop—also facing the cemetery—passed away. My parents eventually purchased that property as well, and we moved in.

Property records tell me I was eleven at the time.

Memory tells a different story.

In my mind, I am six or seven at most—small, exposed, unequipped. Trauma compresses age. Fear makes you younger than you were. When I picture that house, I do not see an eleven-year-old. I see a child.

At first, we were thrilled. No more long afternoons stuck inside the flower shop after school, finishing homework behind the counter while strangers ordered arrangements for funerals we would never attend. Now my brother and I were only a backyard away from "home" while our parents finished closing up.

It felt like freedom.

What none of us realized was that the house came with more than convenience.

It came with something unseen.

Uninvited.

At first, it was subtle—the kind of disturbances you explain away.

A door slamming when no wind stirred. Lights flickering without a blown bulb. The distinct sensation of being watched in an empty room. Whispers that felt less like sound and more like pressure—like breath against the back of your neck.

Then came the sightings.

Shadows where nothing cast them. Movements just beyond peripheral vision. An atmosphere that shifted without warning—thick, charged, oppressive.

And then the dread.

Not cinematic horror. Not dramatic terror.

The slow, gnawing realization that whatever occupied our home had no intention of leaving.

I experienced more in that house than most horror films attempt to portray. There were no orchestral swells or scripted jump scares—only the kind of fear that lingers quietly. The kind that teaches a child to scan rooms before entering them, to sleep lightly, to question what others insist is imagination.

Although each novel discussed in this book draws inspiration from real events, only *Infestation* carries the weight of being directly based on them.

For that reason, Part One leans heavily on excerpts from *Infestation*, weaving fiction with testimony—not to sensationalize what happened, but to give language to what we endured. Fiction allowed me to gather what memory had scattered. It gave structure to moments that once felt chaotic and unnamed.

What follows is a scene from *Infestation*—a fictionalized retelling rooted in one of my earliest memories in that house.

In the novel, I gave my younger self a name: Emma.

Through her eyes, I attempted to process what I witnessed but could not yet understand. Fiction gave me distance. It gave me courage. It allowed me to explore what frightened me without reliving it unfiltered.

The details bend. Dialogue is shaped. Scenes are framed.

But the spine of the story—the fear, the atmosphere, the moment of knowing something was wrong—is real.

An Excerpt from *Infestation*

A BLOOD-CURDLING SCREAM TORE through the house, freezing David in place. He gasped, his heart skipping a beat. "Emma!" The fear in her scream propelled him forward, adrenaline surging through his veins. He sprinted into the living room. Candy, his younger sister, trailed behind him.

"Emmy, what's wrong? Why did you scream?" David asked, gently gripping her shoulders.

Emma's eyes were wide, her body rigid, as if paralyzed by an unseen force.

"Emmy, what's wrong?" he repeated, his voice trembling with concern.

No answer.

David crouched to his knees to meet her gaze. "Emmy, what happened?" he asked.

Still no answer.

He nudged her gently, his voice tinged with urgency. "Answer me, Emmy. Did you see something? In the house?"

She nodded slowly, her vacant eyes fixed on the empty wall in front of her.

He followed her gaze, but there was nothing there. "What did you see?" he asked, his voice now barely above a whisper.

She said nothing, her small frame trembling.

He took her cold hands in his, shaking them gently. "Emmy? What... Did... You... See?"

Finally, she spoke. "It was... It was a man," she whispered, her voice hollow, as though she were in a trance. "His lips were stitched together."

David's heart plummeted, fear clawing at his chest. He quickly scanned the room, then turned to the front door, checking to see if it was still securely locked. It was. But the possibility that someone—something—was still inside the house sent a shiver down his spine. He turned off the television, straining to hear any sound of movement.

The old house creaked and groaned, the soft whispers of the past seeming to echo through the walls. *Did the house always make these sounds?* he wondered, dread tightening its grip on him. *There's no time for questions,* he thought, scooping Emma into his arms. Her tiny heart pounded against his chest like a drum. "Come, Candy," he whispered, reaching for her hand. "Hurry."

"But... my soda!" Candy protested, her voice wavering.

"Shh!" David hissed. "No soda for you." He hurried to the door, the floorboards moaning under his weight. His fingers trembled as he fumbled with the locks, one by one—first, second, third—until the door swung open.

"What about Blue?" Emma whispered, her voice tinged with fear.

"Come on, Blue. Hurry!" he called out softly.

The Chihuahua's ears perked up at the sound of its name, and in an instant, Blue darted off the couch and scurried to David's feet.

Outside, David's eyes scanned the unfamiliar neighborhood, searching for a safe haven. His gaze landed on the nearest house, and with long, purposeful strides, he made his way there.

JOSEPHINE'S HEART PLUMMETED to her stomach when she saw the flashing red and blue lights of a police car parked in her driveway. Panic gripped her chest like a vise, tightening with each breath as a thousand worst-case scenarios raced through her mind. "Oh my God," Josephine muttered, her voice trembling with fear. Desperation fueled her actions as she parked her car haphazardly on the street, flinging the door open and jumping out, not even bothering to close it behind her.

"Aunt Josie, we're over here!" David's voice called out from the neighbor's yard, cutting through the haze of fear clouding Josephine's mind.

Her eyes darted to the porch next door, where she spotted the three children huddled together with the woman who lived there. Relief and terror collided in her chest, creating a whirlwind of emotions that propelled her forward. Her heart pounded as she sprinted toward them, her breath coming in ragged gasps.

"What happened? Is everyone OK?" she asked, her voice shaking as she frantically patted each child, needing to feel their warmth, to know they were unharmed. "Is anyone hurt?"

The children looked up at her, wide-eyed and pale, but seemingly untouched by whatever had brought the police to her home. Josephine's hands shook as she searched their faces for any signs of distress, the fear still gnawing at her insides, refusing to let go.

"We're OK," David assured her, his voice calm despite the tension that hung in the air.

Josephine let out a shaky breath, but her mind still raced, trying to piece together what could have led to this. She looked into the children's faces, searching for answers.

The woman beside them extended her hand. "Hello, my name is Jillian Russo."

"Josephine Perales," she responded, shaking Jillian's hand. Her eyes flicked to her home, her brows knitting in confusion. *I was gone less than twenty minutes!* "What on earth happened?" she asked, her voice heavy with dread.

"Your little girl saw a man, a stranger, in the house," Jillian said.

"WHAT?!" Josephine's voice was sharp with shock, her eyes wide.

"The kids ran over here, and I called 911. The police are inside looking for the man now."

"OK. Thank you for your help," Josephine managed, though her thoughts were a chaotic storm. *I checked the back door before I left. It was locked. I heard David lock the front door—three clicks,* she remembered, her mind scrambling for answers. She turned to David, her voice urgent. "When did this happen? I mean, when *exactly* did this happen?"

"Just a few minutes after you left," he replied. "Emma said she saw a man in the living room. She said his lips were stitched together."

"His lips were stitched together?" Josephine repeated, her confusion deepening. "Did anyone else see him?"

"No, ma'am."

It must be her imagination, Josephine thought, trying to rationalize the bizarre situation. "And where were you? You were supposed to be watching her," she asked, her voice edged with accusation that she immediately regretted.

"I—I was in the kitchen with Candy... cleaning up a spill," David replied, his voice small and guilty. "I heard her scream, and I ran to her as fast as I could."

Josephine took a deep breath, trying to steady herself. "I'm sorry for my tone, David. You did the right thing. Thank you."

"Excuse me, ma'am," a deep, raspy voice interrupted.

Startled, Josephine flinched before turning to see a police officer standing nearby. "Did you find him?" she asked, her anxiety spiking again.

"Is this your home?" the officer asked.

"Yes," she replied quickly. "Did you find him? The man my daughter said she saw?"

"No one is inside the house, ma'am. There's no sign of breaking and entering. We checked every window—they're all secured from the inside." He glanced at the house. "Secured from the outside, too. You know, those burglar bars could be a real issue if there were a fire."

She nodded absently, her mind spinning. "I understand."

"Your daughter—she's young. Your son said—"

"My nephew," she interrupted.

"Your nephew told us your daughter said the man's lips were stitched together. It sounds like she imagined it."

"Momma, I didn't," Emma said, tugging on her blouse. "I saw him. He scared me."

"OK, angel. We'll talk about it later." Josephine turned back to the officer. "Are you sure?" she asked, desperation creeping into her voice.

He nodded. "It's a small house—we checked every inch of it."

"OK," she said, her gaze distant, staring at her home as though it had become a stranger.

"We'll be heading out now," the officer said, turning to David. "But I want you to know you did a good thing by coming to your neighbor's house and having her call us. If it happens again, don't hesitate to do exactly what you did."

They watched in silence as the officers got into their patrol cars and drove off.

"Would you like to come in for a moment?" Jillian asked gently. "Until your husband arrives?"

Josephine brought a trembling hand to her mouth and nodded. "Thank you. Just for a few minutes—to collect my thoughts. I don't want to intrude."

"No problem. Let's go inside."

"Come on, kids," Josephine said, following Jillian into her home.

As they stepped inside, Blue darted between Josephine's legs, brushing against her ankles. She gasped. "Sorry," she stammered. "I'm not normally this—

"Jumpy?" Jillian finished with a sympathetic smile.

Josephine nodded.

"I don't blame you. I'd feel the same way if I came home to find my child with a stranger and the police outside my house," Jillian said. "Please, take a seat anywhere you'd like."

"Thank you," Josephine said, settling on the couch as the kids made themselves comfortable in Jillian's son's room.

The sound of children's laughter filled the air, but Josephine was lost in her thoughts. *I wasn't gone long. How could someone have gotten in? And why was Emma the only one who saw him? She must have imagined it. It's the only explanation.*

"Can I get you some coffee?" Jillian asked, breaking through her thoughts.

"What?" Josephine blinked, momentarily disoriented.

"Coffee? Can I get you some?"

"No, thank you."

"If you don't mind me asking—what's on your mind?"

Josephine hesitated, unsure whether to spill her worries to a woman she barely knew. But the need to voice her fears overpowered her reservations. She looked at Jillian, her eyes searching for understanding.

"It's just that Emma, she's not like other kids. She's honest and smart—very smart. I know every parent says that about their child, so you'll have to take my word for it. And she's never had a wild imagination... At least, she never did before."

She paused, her thoughts tangled.

"I'm sorry, I shouldn't be going on like this. I'm expecting my husband home any minute." She stood up, ready to leave. "Thanks again for your help today."

"Josephine? Before you go?"

"Yes?"

"I know it's none of my business, so what I'm about to say—well, it could go in one ear and out the other."

"Please, go ahead," Josephine said, focusing on Jillian. "I'm listening."

"It's just, in my experience, kids—especially the honest, smart ones like your little girl—don't have a history of imagining things. They don't tend to become liars and start imagining things overnight."

Reflection

In the excerpt you've just read, young Emma sensed what most adults would have dismissed without a second thought. Her reaction was not rooted in weakness or fearfulness—it came from sensitivity. From a spiritual awareness not yet dulled by skepticism, routine, or the demand for rational explanation. Children like Emma are not easily deceived. They see what is real, often with startling clarity, even when the rest of us are too busy, too guarded, or too distracted to notice.

And the enemy knows this.

It does not wait for them to grow older. It targets them early. It seeks out the sensitive—the perceptive, the spiritually open—and attempts to silence them before discernment can fully take root. It sows confusion before truth has language. It plants doubt before faith has framework. It tries to make them question what they know—deeply, intuitively, purely—before they ever learn to trust their own spirit.

I know this because I lived it.

I was four years old when my father was asked to officiate the funeral service of a man whose death was cloaked in whispers and quiet horror. I didn't understand it then, but his body had been used as part of a satanic ritual—brutal, intentional, and unspeakably dark. The details were so disturbing that the casket remained sealed. No one was allowed to see the body. No one wanted to.

The next day, my parents stepped out for a quick grocery run, leaving me at home with my fifteen-year-old sister. It was nothing out of the ordinary. They were never gone long, and it had never been a problem before. The afternoon was calm and uneventful—just the two of us in the house. I was playing quietly in the bedroom I shared with my sister while she watched television in the living room.

And then something shifted.

Even now, it is difficult to find the right words for what happened next. The air seemed to thicken, as if the room itself had taken a breath and held it. The house grew unnaturally quiet. Time slowed. Sound dulled. I turned instinctively toward the doorway—and froze.

Something was standing there.

A stranger. Perfectly still. Too still. Watching me.

But it wasn't just what I saw. It was what I felt. A presence so heavy it pressed into the walls, seeped into the floor, and made my very soul recoil. Darkness didn't merely fill the space—it asserted itself. It crowded the room. It demanded attention.

Whatever stood in that doorway was not of this world. And somehow—as young as I was—I knew it.

At first, I couldn't scream. The fear was too sharp, too sudden—lodged in my throat like barbed wire. My lungs refused to cooperate, as though my body itself was bracing against something it could not comprehend. When my voice finally broke free, it wasn't a scream in the usual sense. It was raw. Primal. Torn from a place deeper than fear itself.

Later, my sister would tell me it didn't even sound like me.

Because I wasn't screaming at a man.

I was screaming at something that should not have been there.

Whatever stood in that doorway had not been invited. It was not alive. And I knew it with a certainty that did not require explanation.

When I told my sister what I had seen, she didn't question me. She didn't laugh it off or reduce it to imagination or a bad dream. She saw my face. She heard the scream that still echoed in the room. And without hesitation, she grabbed my hand.

We ran—barefoot and breathless—out of the house and into the yard, leaving everything behind except the certainty that something had crossed a line it was never meant to cross.

We were standing on the lawn, hearts pounding, when our parents pulled into the driveway. My sister rushed to them, gasping out what I said I had seen.

Without a word, my father sprinted into the house. Every door. Every window. Every closet. He checked it all. Finding no one, he asked questions:

What did the stranger look like?

What was he wearing?

Was he short or tall?

Thin or heavy?

Hair? Short or long?

I still remember what I told my father.

He was dressed in black—tall and thin. His hair was neither short nor long, not truly hair at all. He was bald. The details came to me with unsettling clarity, as if I were describing someone standing just beyond the edge of the room.

My answers left my father stunned—but not entirely surprised. Without saying a word, he reached for the obituary section of the local newspaper and held it out in front of me. There, staring back in stark black and white, was the man I had just described. The same man I had seen. The same man whose funeral we had only moments earlier attended.

My father didn't press me for more. He didn't question me, didn't attempt to reason it away or soften it with logic. And that restraint meant something—because over the years, whether fairly or not, he would come to doubt me plenty.

I learned to recognize the look in his eyes when skepticism took root as clearly as I knew the lines of my own hand.

But not that day. That day, in that quiet, unguarded moment, he believed me—fully and without hesitation. And somehow, that belief was both a comfort and a confirmation of the very thing I wished were not true.

That moment as a child—when fear pressed in so tightly that my voice vanished, when even screaming felt impossible—was also the moment I began to understand that spiritual warfare is not a distant theological idea or a dramatic metaphor reserved for Scripture alone.

It is real. It is present. And it is daily.

Whether we acknowledge it or not, our children often stand on the front lines of it.

That is why we cannot afford to dismiss their visions, their dreams, or their unshakable gut feelings. We must resist the urge to explain away what unsettles us simply because it challenges our comfort. Instead of teaching our children to ignore what they see or feel, we must equip them to face it—to recognize it, to respond to it, and to stand firm within it.

We must teach them to speak the name of Jesus without fear. To understand that authority is not earned by age or strength, but granted by God. Even in their smallness, they carry His power.

Because evil does not wait for them to grow up before taking interest in them. And neither does God.

> "Then Elisha prayed and said, 'O Lord, please open his eyes that he may see.' So the Lord opened the eyes of the young man, and he saw, and behold, the mountain was full of horses and chariots of fire all around Elisha."
>
> 2 Kings 6:17 (ESV)

Chapter 2

The Vulnerable

W hen my brother and I first voiced our concerns about moving into the house across from the cemetery, our parents brushed it off. "The dead are gone. They can't hurt you," they would say. "It's the living you should be worried about."

They weren't wrong.

It took years for me to realize that the cemetery across the street was never the threat. I never saw a ghost drifting between gravestones, never heard the clink of chains in the night air.

Evil doesn't always arrive as ghosts or goblins. In fact, it rarely does. It doesn't often storm through the front door. Evil seeps in, slow and deliberate, like water seeking the smallest crack. It studies you. Waits for the moment you're tired, distracted, or wounded. Then it slips through, unseen, and settles deep—working undisturbed.

That's the danger.

Not the noise. Not the spectacle. But the quiet, calculated way it chooses its prey.

When evil disguises itself as compassion—when it wears a friendly face, speaks through a family member, or wraps itself in our best intentions—it becomes harder to name. Harder to resist. And dangerously easy to welcome in. It seeps through unnoticed cracks—through exhaustion, distraction, doubt. It slips past when we're too tired to question the knock at the door, too busy to examine what feels wrong, or so desperate for relief that we can't tell the difference between help and harm.

Evil doesn't always bare its teeth. Sometimes it speaks in half-truths. It smiles sweetly. It cloaks itself in grief. It soothes as it schemes. And sometimes—like in the excerpt you're about to read—it arrives dressed as kindness. A good deed. A loving act. Like a compassionate couple welcoming their troubled young niece into their home, hoping love might be louder than the voices she hears.

The scene from Infestation that follows is drawn from real events. Only the names have been changed.

An Excerpt from *Infestation*

"MOMMA, HAVE YOU SEEN BLUE?" Emma asked, clutching her handy-dandy notebook.

"She's right next to you," her mother replied, smiling as the real-life puppy pitter-pattered at Emma's feet.

"No, I mean my *stuffy*, not the real one! I can't find it anywhere!"

"Emmy, hurry! Your cartoon is about to start!" David called from the living room.

"Momma, I *need* Blue! My show's starting!" she cried.

"I'm sorry, angel... Momma has her hands full. We have company coming today."

"Emmy! It's starting!"

"Momma! Please!" she begged. "You *know* I can't watch *Blue's Clues* without Blue!"

Her mother paused, thinking. Then her face lit up. "I placed it in the toy chest in your room."

"OK, thanks, Momma!" Emma chirped, skipping down the hallway. She reached her bedroom door—but the knob wouldn't turn.

"Candy? We're not supposed to lock doors!" she called, knocking.

"Emmy? Candy? Are you in there?" David's voice echoed from the other room, but she didn't answer. A spark of determination lit her eyes.

With her pup by her side, Emma ran to her parents' bedroom and ducked into the shared closet that connected their rooms. Blue's tiny legs scrambled to keep up.

"Come on, Blue," she whispered, scooping her puppy into her arms. "I need to get my other Blue." The pup tilted its head in confusion. "You *know* what I mean."

She pushed through hanging clothes, reaching the far side of the closet, and opened the door to her room.

And froze.

Candy was standing there.

Waiting.

Watching.

"Leave," Candy said coldly, her body looming over the child like a shadow.

"I just need my—"

Without warning, Candy's hands closed around Emma's neck like a vice. In one fluid, unnatural motion, she lifted her off the ground with terrifying ease. Emma's puppy slipped from her arms, hitting the floor with a soft thud.

Emma's legs thrashed wildly, her shoes scraping at nothing. She tried to scream—but no sound escaped. Only the widening panic in her eyes betrayed the silent struggle for air.

Candy's face twisted, her eyes hollow. Her mouth curled unnaturally, as if something else had taken over.

Emma clawed at Candy's hands, her vision blurring.

Then—a *bark*. A desperate, frantic yelping.

"Emmy? Candy?" David called from outside, jiggling the doorknob.

Emma's eyes moved toward the door. She tried to scream again, but it was no use.

DAVID'S INSTINCTS WERE ON HIGH gear. *I have to get in there*, he thought. The sound of splintering wood echoed through the house as David delivered a powerful kick to the door. The door's aged, rusty hinges groaned in protest, not giving in.

"David? What's going on over there?" Aunt Josie called out from the kitchen.

No time to explain, he thought, as he stepped back and propelled himself forward, slamming his shoulder into the door. Still, it did not give. Emma's secret tunnel, he thought. With bated breath, he sprinted into the next room and plunged through the depths of the adjoining closet, his body contorting to fit the small space. Time seemed to slow as the darkness swallowed him whole, but he pushed through, crawling with a speed fueled by fear. He emerged on the other side to find his sister's hands wrapped tightly around Emma's tiny neck.

"Candy, stop! Let her go!" David shouted as Aunt Josie pounded on the door demanding to be let in.

At last, Candy released her grip. Emma fell on the bed, desperately gasping for air as David stepped inside.

"Oh my God," Aunt Josie said, following David in.

Emma was breathless, her face pale.

"Angel, are you OK?" Aunt Josie asked.

Emma inhaled deeply, struggling to fight back tears, and nodded.

Aunt Josie turned to David. "How did you know?" she asked.

At a loss for words, he shrugged.

Aunt Josie locked eyes with him with a piercing gaze. "Two minutes ago, Emma was in the kitchen with me, searching for her stuffed animal. I didn't hear a thing. How did you know she was in danger?"

"I don't know," he replied. "It's just, Emmy didn't come when I called her... And I know how much she loves her show... And I didn't know where Candy was, and sometimes she doesn't know her own strength... And then I heard Blue barking... And the door was locked," he said, his words tumbling out in a rush as panic crept into his voice. "I'm sorry, Aunt Josie. I'm really, really sorry."

"Don't be. You just saved my baby's life," she said, squeezing Emma in an embrace.

Reflection

There is no easy way to process an attack like I endured—not as a child living it, and not as an adult revisiting it. It took me decades to speak openly about it—first through metaphor, then through fiction, and finally now, in my own voice.

Even as I write these words, there's a familiar weight in my chest. Not from lingering fear, but from recognition—because trauma doesn't dissolve. It burrows into your bones. It weaves itself into your memories. And when it resurfaces, it doesn't ask permission.

But my parents believed in redemption. They believed that no one was beyond the reach of love or the healing power of faith. So when the opportunity came to welcome someone broken into our home—someone who had suffered, someone who had been cast aside—they opened the door with open arms and open hearts.

They had hoped that a warm bed, a steady routine, and a house filled with prayer and stability might help repair what life had fractured. That love, structure, and grace could change the trajectory of a wounded life.

But what they didn't know—what none of us could have known—was what those voices were really saying in the quiet corners of this young relative's mind. Or what they might one day persuade her to do. They couldn't have predicted how deeply spiritual torment can hide behind a child's smile. How persistent it can be. How patient.

That moment—the one I never saw coming—changed me forever. I was attacked by someone I never would have imagined capable of such harm, someone whose face I had associated with innocence. In an instant, I saw what evil could do when it hides behind a smile. It didn't just shatter my sense of safety; it dismantled the foundation of how I understood trust. In its place, it built a sharper, more unflinching awareness of spiritual warfare.

I began to understand that evil is not always theatrical. It doesn't always announce itself with slammed doors, rattling walls, or screams in the night.

More often, it is patient. It seeps in quietly—through grief, through wounds left untended, through doors left unlocked because no one imagined a threat could enter there.

Sometimes, evil arrives wearing the face of someone you've known since childhood. Sometimes, it hides in sympathy, in softness, in the noble act of helping. And that's what makes it so dangerous. Because when evil comes disguised as mercy, it's easier to miss. Easier to excuse. Easier to welcome in. But what I've learned since that day is this:

Discernment is as vital as compassion. Faith must be partnered with wisdom.

And while we're called to love the broken, we must also remain spiritually vigilant. Because the enemy doesn't always come charging. Sometimes... it simply asks for a place to stay.

Had someone not come storming into that room to save me that day—or had they arrived even a moment too late—I would not be here today. Some call it chance—I call it a miracle. But that moment taught me something more:

God still performs miracles, and He still sends protectors.

They may not arrive with flaming swords or part seas with a staff. They may not resemble angels, prophets, or warriors from the pages of Scripture. In fact, they rarely look like the people you expect—the ones you've been taught to honor, admire, or depend on.

The truth is, Jesus still works miracles today, and the Holy Spirit still moves through ordinary people doing extraordinary things. Sometimes a protector comes disguised as a distant friend who calls at just the right time, a stranger who offers unexpected kindness, or a loved one whose steady presence anchors you when the world feels like it's falling apart.

Scripture reminds us of Rahab, a prostitute in Jericho, who hid the Israelite spies and saved them from certain death. To the world, she didn't look like a protector—but she was one. God chose her because the Holy Spirit doesn't look for *ability*. It looks for *availability*. And when someone, however unlikely, becomes that vessel, the miraculous breaks through.

Chosen.

Positioned.

Brave.

What happened that day could have ended in heartbreak. But it ended in *deliverance*.

That's the thing about God's help—it rarely comes wrapped in the packaging we expect. But if you're paying attention, you'll see it: the quiet interventions, the timely words, the people placed in your path not by coincidence but by divine appointment.

Sometimes they come in the form of a scrappy little dog with a bark that won't quit. Sometimes they appear as strangers who act on instinct, even before understanding the danger. And sometimes, they speak through that still, small voice—the one that nudges you when something feels off and whispers, "*Go. Check on them. Now.*"

Scripture reminds us:

> "Behold, I have given you authority to tread on serpents and scorpions, and over all the power of the enemy, and nothing shall hurt you."
>
> Luke 10:19 (ESV)

Chapter 3

The Doubted

I t happens without warning...

   You see something you never expected—something that should not be—and the world tilts. Maybe it's in the flicker of a shadow where no one stands. Maybe it's in the words you never imagined hearing from someone you love. Maybe it's in the thing your spouse did that you swore they never could.

At first, you blame yourself. Your eyes must be playing tricks. Your mind, your emotions—overreacting. Then someone tells you it's nothing. Just your imagination.

That's where doubt takes root—quiet, subtle, invasive. It creeps into the spaces between what you saw and what you're told.

It starts small, but it grows, fed by fear, by wounds you've carried too long, or by something far darker. Evil doesn't need your full belief. It only needs a crack. Just enough to slip through and start dismantling your confidence, your discernment, your spiritual clarity.

The story that follows begins with Emma, a girl confronted by something both familiar and deeply wrong. It may read like fiction. But it echoes something far more real. Because whether the attack comes as an action, a whisper, a shadow, or a child's toy turned unholy, the damage is the same.

An Excerpt from *Infestation*

EMMA CLUTCHED HER LOYAL, floppy-eared, white-furred stuffed animal—a puppy dog named *Blue*—held tight as she narrowed her gaze on the colorful snake slithering across the page of the book her father was reading to her. The snake moved with a friendly, approachable grace, but its wide, innocent-looking eyes held a glint of wickedness, hinting at its true nature.

Emma hung on every word as her father recounted the tale of how Satan had once been the most beautiful angel. But he didn't want to be just an angel—he wanted to be God. Filled with resentment and hatred, Satan was cast out of heaven. In the Garden of Eden, God gave Adam and Eve just one rule: don't eat the fruit of the Tree of Knowledge. But Satan, determined to disrupt God's plan, disguised himself as a snake and waited in the garden to trick Adam and Eve into eating the forbidden fruit.

"How did he do that?" Emma asked, her brow furrowing.

"Do what?" her father replied.

"How did he disguise himself as a snake? They didn't have costumes back then."

He smiled gently. "It was an evil magic trick."

She pondered this for a moment, then asked, "If he wanted to trick them, why did he choose a snake? Why not something less scary, like a bunny?"

Her father chuckled. "It wouldn't have mattered. They wouldn't have been afraid anyway. They didn't even know what fear was."

Emma's mind raced with questions. Why were Adam and Eve naked in the first place? How did the snake talk to them? Did he move his mouth? There were so many trees in the garden and so much to eat—why did they choose the one tree they weren't supposed to touch? And if that tree was so bad, why did God create it? She glanced out the window at the darkness outside, knowing there wasn't enough time for all her questions. She settled on one.

"Why didn't God just not make that tree in the first place?"

Her father nodded thoughtfully. "You know what poison ivy is, right?"

Emma nodded vigorously, recalling her class field trip to the Chicago Botanic Garden when her teacher warned them not to touch it. One of her classmates, Aiden, thought it would be funny to touch it with as many parts of his body as possible. "That's why an ambulance took Aiden to the hospital."

"Exactly," her father said. "But do you know what would happen if there was no poison ivy?"

"Aiden wouldn't have gone to the hospital," she replied confidently.

Her father laughed softly. "Maybe, but also, birds like robins, which feed on its berries, would have nothing to eat. Dirt would run off slopes and fill riverbanks, leaving many animals without water to drink, and we wouldn't have some of the medicines we have today."

Emma's eyes moved rapidly as she processed the information. "I think I understand now, Daddy."

Her father leaned over and kissed her forehead. "Sweet dreams," he said as he stood up to leave.

Emma whispered a prayer as her father stepped out of the room. "Now I lay me down to sleep, I pray the Lord my soul to keep; keep me safe through the night and wake me with the morning light. If I should die before I wake, I pray the Lord my soul to take. Amen." She closed her eyes, ready to drift off to dreamland.

Her eyelids fluttered open as the room suddenly filled with a cacophony of mechanical whirs and electronic melodies. The darkness was pierced by colorful lights flashing from her toys.

"Oh no," Emma whispered, climbing out of bed. "You'll wake Momma and Daddy."

Her heart raced as she ran to quiet the toys, one by one.

As she turned toward an unfamiliar sound—a haunting eerie laughter—her gaze settled on her father's prized toy, Tickle Me Elmo. He had gotten it for her as a housewarming present. She didn't care much for it, thinking herself too old for such a baby toy. But her father had spent hours waiting in line at the toy store and took pride in bringing it home. So, she had accepted it with a smile and placed it on her shelf, never to be played with.

Cautiously, Emma approached the doll.

Maybe it needs new batteries, she thought, picking up the red plush figure.

She placed the doll face down on her lap and carefully peeled back the Velcro from its back. With a gentle click, she deactivated the battery pack.

"There," she whispered, returning the doll to its seated position on the shelf.

As she climbed back into bed, an eerie, distant giggle filled the room. Emma's eyes widened in terror as she slowly turned her gaze back to the doll. It was standing now, its large, round eyes glowing like two bright orbs. The doll cackled, its twisted laughter a dark parody of the innocent giggle it was meant to have.

Emma stared at the toy, her heart pounding in her chest. She swallowed hard as the reality of what was happening began to sink in.

It's not supposed to stand like that. Its eyes aren't supposed to glow like that.

The toy extended its fuzzy, vibrant red arm toward her. Its mouth moved in puppet fashion as it said, "Does Emma wanna be Elmo's friiiend?"

She gasped as another realization settled in.

Its mouth isn't supposed to move like that.

It cackled again, its body trembling—the one thing it was designed to do. The trembling stopped abruptly. The puppet opened its mouth wide. "Plllleeeease."

With a grotesque burst, a torrent of roaches erupted from the darkness of its mouth, their wings beating frantically, as though they were multiplying in the depths of its belly, waiting to break free. She opened her mouth to scream, but fear gripped her, and no sound escaped.

Reflection

The enemy hides in the ordinary. He wears what we love. He settles into what feels safe, familiar, even comforting. He thrives in confusion and feeds on silence. And when doubt finally blooms, it doesn't merely cause you to question what you saw—it compels you to question who you are.

The excerpt you've just read—Emma and the possessed toy—may strike some as exaggerated, even symbolic. But for those who have lived through genuine spiritual warfare—for those who have felt the veil thin, who have sensed an unseen presence lingering just beyond the edge of sight, who have encountered moments that logic refuses to contain—these stories do not need embellishment. If anything, they demand restraint. Because the truth, when it finally surfaces, is often far more terrifying—and far more powerful—than fiction could ever be.

There is always a reckoning after you brush against the edges of darkness. A moment when something deep within your soul recognizes the truth before your mind has words for it. You saw something. You felt something. You knew—instinctively, unmistakably—that it was not right. And yet, almost immediately, your mind begins to claw for escape routes. A way to unsee it. To unfeel it. To make it smaller, safer, explainable.

And then comes the voice.

The voice of reason. Sometimes the voice of authority. Sometimes the voice of someone you trust.

They offer another explanation—one that soothes rather than confronts, that comforts rather than convicts. A softer story. A safer narrative. And you want to believe it, because the alternative demands too much courage. It requires you to acknowledge that the world is not as contained or predictable as you hoped. That there are forces at work beyond what the eyes can see.

And just like that, conviction bends. Certainty blurs. What was once clear becomes questionable. Second-guessing slips in and quietly takes its place.

This is how the enemy most often works—not through spectacle, but through subtle subversion. Not always by possessing a body or manifesting in dramatic displays, but by eroding trust from the inside out. Sometimes all he needs is your doubt. A brief hesitation. A pause in belief. A single seed planted quietly in the soil of fear.

That seed is dangerous—not because it shouts, but because it whispers. Because it slowly suffocates the confidence you once had. Doubt doesn't need a megaphone. It only needs you to stop trusting what you already know to be true.

Emma's encounter was never about a toy gone wrong. It was a spiritual confrontation—carefully cloaked in something so familiar, so innocent, that it nearly went unnoticed. And that is the battle we so often miss. We look for darkness in the obvious places, while it disguises itself in the ordinary.

As I reflect on this chapter, I am reminded that whether an experience is believed to be real or not, its consequences always are. The fear is real. The silence that follows is real. The spiritual confusion that lingers is real. These moments leave marks, shaping how we see the world and ourselves within it.

And the enemy is real—using every tool available to him, including dreams, imagination, memory, and our most closely guarded fears, to make us forget who we are and what we carry.

But we are not left defenseless.

Doubt may be his weapon, but truth is our shield. And when we speak that truth—when we dare to bring light into the shadows—we begin to reclaim what fear tried to steal. We remember our authority. We remember our identity. And we remember that darkness, no matter how cleverly disguised, has never been stronger than the light.

> "Be sober-minded; be watchful. Your adversary the devil prowls
> around like a roaring lion, seeking someone to devour."
>
> 1 Peter 5:8 (ESV)

Doubt may be the enemy's first tactic. But it doesn't have to be the final word. So if you've ever seen what others couldn't... felt something no one else believed... carried a story in silence for fear of being misunderstood...

You are not alone. You are not broken. You are not imagining things. *You are likely more spiritually attuned than the world dares to admit.*

And that is no accident. Because those who see are not merely witnesses. They are the ones called to stand.

Chapter 4

The Intruders

W hat happens when the darkness doesn't knock because it's already inside? When my family moved into the house across the street from the cemetery, we thought we were gaining convenience—not company. But it didn't take long for my brother and me to realize we weren't alone.

It started small. A flicker in the corner of an eye. A faint sound where none should be. The heavy weight of being watched, even in an empty room. Then came the apparitions—shifting shapes that materialized in different forms: a dense fog in the middle of the room, a little girl standing at the foot of the bed.

We saw things. Heard things. Felt things. What we experienced wasn't just unsettling—it was undeniable. And no matter how many times the lights were checked or the doors relocked, the feeling never left. The darkness hadn't followed us in. It had been waiting all along.

In time, the rest of my family would come to witness what my brother and I already knew. But it began with us—the children. And that's why I believe children can see what adults no longer can. Before the filters. Before the doubt. Before the world trains them to explain away the unexplainable—they are wide open. Spiritually awake. Untouched by the numbing weight of reason. What they see is not always the stuff of make-believe.

Sometimes, it's the truth we've lost the eyes to recognize. And in that house... What we saw was looking back at us. The spiritual oppression we felt as children, the fear that chased us from one end of the yard to the other, the sense that something ancient and malevolent had claimed the space long before we arrived... All of it is etched into my memory.

An Excerpt from *Infestation*

JILLIAN'S EYES NARROWED AS SHE thought about her family, the implications of Daniel's question slowly dawning on her. She had visited the family plot with her father countless times over the years. Her grandparents and uncle were buried alongside her uncle's girlfriend, their names etched together on a single black granite gravestone.

"My uncle's name was Michael David Marino," Jillian said, her voice heavy with realization. "He was named after my grandfather, who died in the car with him."

Josephine's eyes widened. "Could it really have been your uncle who was the original target of the revenge spell?" she asked.

Having lived in Hillside all her life, Jillian knew what every Hillside Elementary student learned—Hillside began as a village in 1905, named after the Illinois Central Railroad stop. The name came from the uphill climb the westbound trains had to make in that area. She also knew that residential development started in the 1920s, and by 1940, the population was just over a thousand.

"Hillside was so small back then—how many teenagers named Michael David could there have been?" Jillian said, a mix of sorrow and frustration in her voice.

"I'm sorry," Daniel said gently. "This must be difficult to hear."

Jillian's heart ached for her father, who had lost his entire family in such a tragic way. She couldn't even begin to fathom the depth of his pain, being left utterly alone in the aftermath. Her thoughts drifted to Candy, so young and innocent, caught in the crossfire of forces far beyond her comprehension. The weight of it all pressed down on Jillian, overwhelming her with emotion. With tears welling in her eyes, she stepped up to Emmanuel, her voice trembling with grief and disbelief.

"How could this happen?" she whispered, the anguish evident in every word.

"The spell, the evil—it's very powerful," Emmanuel replied.

"That's not what I meant," she said, her gaze intense and fiery. "You're a pastor—how could God allow this to happen? And under your own roof?"

Emmanuel straightened his posture and locked eyes with her. "Jillian, I know you're angry—I am too. But God did not allow this to happen. Satan did."

She broke away from his gaze, crossing her arms as he continued. "You must understand, the war between good and evil, angels and demons—it's not conceptual, not a myth or legend. It's very real." He stepped closer, his voice steady and firm. "Do you understand that?"

"I guess I don't," Jillian admitted, her voice tinged with frustration and confusion. She had learned long ago in church that God gave His children free will and that evil could cloud judgment, leading to bad choices. People weren't robots; when they made decisions—like invoking evil spirits—terrible consequences were often inevitable. But what happened to Candy didn't make sense. And if she was going to use her gift to fulfill a higher purpose, she needed to understand.

Daniel stepped up to her, his expression compassionate. "I think I can help explain."

She turned to him, searching for clarity. "I'm listening."

"Jillian, God didn't conjure up the evil responsible for what happened," he began, his tone gentle but firm. "The people who unleashed this, the ones who conjured the spell—they are responsible. Whether they knew it or not, whether they intended it or not, they did this. They toyed with dark forces and, in doing so, became soldiers for evil. Their actions unleashed something so corrupt that it not only took your uncle and his girlfriend but also your grandparents, and now Candy—even after all these years. And if we don't stop it, no one will."

Soldiers for evil. His words ignited her imagination: she envisioned armies locked in battle—one side driven by darkness, fueled by desires for revenge and chaos, spreading havoc across the world. The other side, a force for good, striving to contain and extinguish the darkness, to prevent it from consuming everything. And then there were the inevitable casualties—innocent lives, like Candy's, caught in the crossfire of this relentless struggle. The thought made her angry. So angry that it stirred something deep within her—a fierce determination to join the battle for good.

"I hope that helps," Daniel said. "It's what made me understand why sometimes bad things happen to the best of people—good, innocent people. And it's what makes me that much more committed to fighting the good fight."

She took a deep breath. "Yes, it helps." With an intense glare, she turned to Emmanuel and said, "Now, how are we going to fight this thing?"

Emmanuel appeared focused yet distant, his gaze locked onto hers, as though calculating something in his mind.

"It couldn't hurt," Daniel said, picking up on the intensity in her voice. "It's a powerful spell—we may need the help."

But Jillian knew it was Emmanuel who had the final say in the matter. Suspense hung heavy in the air as she awaited his response.

Emmanuel eyed Jillian up and down, as though silently weighing her resolve. "You are of strong spirit—"

"Yes," she interrupted confidently.

"That wasn't a question," he replied, his tone firm. "As I was saying, you are of strong spirit, so you may stay."

Jillian's eyes lit up with excitement.

"But let's be clear," Emmanuel continued. "We're not putting on a show here. I'm allowing you to stay because I want you to recognize how valuable your gift is and learn to wield it—not fear it."

HE COULDN'T HEAR WHAT Jillian could, but he didn't need to. The silence had lingered too long, and Emmanuel's experience told him it was a deliberate tactic. The demon was hiding, hoping that if it remained quiet enough, they might leave it undisturbed.

But Emmanuel wasn't fooled. He could feel evil seeping from the shadows, like the stench of a rotting carcass unearthed from a shallow grave. He stepped into David's room, where the final two corners of the home awaited consecration. As he entered, he began to recite prayers of deliverance, his voice firm and unwavering.

"I renounce and rebuke all witchcraft, occult practices, divination, and sorcery that were made in this room in Jesus' name!" Emmanuel exclaimed, anointing the room's corner with oil.

The air crackled with an intense energy, and the light bulbs throughout the house exploded in a violent symphony of shattered glass, as if the very walls were rebelling against his words. The house plunged into darkness, save for the small, flickering flame in Jillian's hands.

Daniel flinched, instinctively raising his arms to shield Jillian from the shower of glass shards raining down around them. As the echo of the explosions faded into silence, he turned to her with a wry smile. "Must have hit a sore spot," he said, his voice a mix of tension and grim humor.

"I destroy all demonic activity and every demonic thought that has ever been opened in this home. I shut it down in the name of Jesus Christ!" Emmanuel declared.

Voices growled and croaked through the darkness like grizzly bears disturbed from their slumber.

"I can hear them now," Daniel said. "We must be getting close."

Emmanuel pressed on. "I renounce any allegiances to the kingdom of darkness and Satan made in this home in Jesus' name!"

The croaking grew louder, competing to drown out his commands, and the room grew colder as the demonic energy drained it of heat.

"Satan, you have no power over us! You have no power over God's kingdom!"

Reflection

In the excerpt you just read, I offered a glimpse into the beginnings of the darkness that settled in our home. The truth is, I don't think we ever truly uncovered where it came from—or why it chose us. But in time, its presence was undeniable. And my father was not the kind of man to ignore the undeniable.

What you've just read is drawn from his real actions—the night he took his stand, stepped into the shadows, and confronted what could not be seen with the only weapons he knew would work: his faith, his authority, his resolve to drive the darkness out. Like Emmanuel in *Avīci Sagga*, my father walked from room to room—Bible in one hand, anointing oil in the other—declaring what had permission to stay and what did not.

He didn't whisper his prayers. He spoke them aloud, boldly, with authority, marking every window, every doorway, every corner of that house with the name of Jesus. And when my father prayed over every doorway and window, he wasn't just reciting scripture—he was waging war. He was engaging in spiritual battle, refusing to surrender sacred ground. With every bold declaration, he drew a line in the sand and stood on the truth:

Our home belongs to God. And darkness has no place here.

And we felt it. My brother and I would look at each other and just... know. The air shifted.

The fear lifted.

But unlike what you see in the movies, nothing changed overnight.

The shadows didn't vanish all at once. Prayer services moved from the church into our living room. The church band shifted rehearsals to our home. Praise music played on the stereo even when we weren't there—songs of deliverance and freedom pulsing through the speakers like a spiritual heartbeat.

Slowly—deliberately—through prayer and persistence, something sacred began to take root. My father didn't just cleanse the space...

God claimed it.

Scripture tells us:

"And when they began to sing and praise, the LORD set an
ambush against the men of Ammon, Moab, and Mount Seir,
who had come against Judah, so that they were routed. "

2 Chronicles 20:22 (ESV)

Worship is not mere expression—it is a *weapon.* It is battle in its purest form.
Evil feeds on fear, chaos, and silence, but worship disrupts its hold. When we
lift our voices, we are not just singing; we are building a throne for the presence
of God to reign.

Worship restores order. It floods the darkness with light. It proclaims truth
until lies scatter. Like a flame struck in the heart of the night, it exposes every
hidden thing—and drives it out. Where God is enthroned, darkness cannot
remain. No demonic spirit lingers in a house, a heart, or a life drenched in praise.

When you're under spiritual attack, it's easy to focus on the fear—to obsess
over the shadows. But worship lifts your gaze. It shifts your focus from the battle
to the One who has already won it. And that shift is everything. That shift is
power. Worship realigns the atmosphere. Prayer fortifies it. And faith, spoken
aloud, sends the enemy running.

Looking back, our house became a sanctuary. And with that, the heaviness
broke. The noises stopped. The shadows disappeared. The apparitions moved
out. Decades later, my parents still live in that house—and not one of us has
seen another spirit since. I now understand we have authority over the spiritual
atmosphere of our homes. Fear doesn't get the final word. Darkness doesn't get
to linger where faith is active and alive.

What began as one of the most terrifying seasons of my childhood became
one of the most important spiritual lessons of my life:

Your home is holy ground. But you have to claim it.

Chapter 5

The Devil's Foothold

E ven after we had lived through a haunting that left a permanent imprint on both of us—something that awakened a spiritual sensitivity in me that never faded—my older brother still chose to toy with the very thing we had been warned against.

He played with a spirit board.

Not at a friend's house. Not at a careless sleepover. But in our home.

The same home we had prayed over.

Anointed.

Declared sacred ground.

The place we believed—after months of turmoil, fear, and relentless prayer—had finally been reclaimed for peace.

It hadn't.

By the time I had begun to feel safe again within those walls, my brother's ordeal was only beginning. Long after the disturbances had stopped for me, he began seeing spirits again. At first, no one knew. He carried it quietly, alone, burdened by something he did not yet understand and likely did not want to name.

But the change in him could not stay hidden.

Once the pride of his class—brilliant, disciplined, quick-witted—he began to unravel. Restlessness replaced focus. Irritability replaced confidence. The brother we had known so well seemed to be slipping away, piece by piece.

His temper flared without warning. His laughter vanished. He grew distant, defensive, and unpredictable.

A heaviness clung to him, as though something unseen had fastened itself to his spirit.

His eyes told the story before his words ever did. Once bright with mischief and intelligence, they dulled, their light receding into shadow. His expression hardened. His patience thinned to nothing. He lashed out over small things, then withdrew altogether, isolating himself from the family that loved him. Slowly, painfully, he became someone we did not recognize.

This was not teenage moodiness. This was not rebellion. This was not a phase.

What we were witnessing was oppression—an external weight pressing inward, hollowing out the brother I once knew.

And then there was the smell...

Not the ordinary, unpleasant odors of adolescence. This was something else entirely. A thick, sulfuric stench—rotten, unmistakable—clung to him. It seeped into his clothes. It lingered in his bedroom. It hung in the air long after he passed through a room. It was as if something unseen followed him, leaving its mark behind, announcing its presence without shame.

My father noticed. We all did.

My father was disappointed—but not panicked. His response was not emotional or frantic. Instead, there was a shift in his posture, a heaviness in his bearing—a gravity I had seen only a handful of times in my life. He understood exactly what was happening. He recognized the signs. He knew which spiritual doors had been opened and the kind of invitation that had been extended.

He knew the enemy rarely forces entry. He waits to be welcomed.

An Excerpt from *Infestation*

"IT'S HARD TO TELL WHAT we're dealing with here," Emmanuel said. "There's not exactly a sign-in sheet for this."

Unamused, Josephine glared at him. "Give me a number. Ballpark—how many demons?"

Emmanuel inhaled deeply as he considered how to answer her question. "Between what Emma has experienced, the banging, the wall heater, Candy, and likely even the roach infestation—"

"What do the roaches have to do with anything?"

"Roaches—particularly the kind that can eat through a newly replaced window frame overnight—are a symptom of diabolical infestation."

Stunned, Josephine placed her hand over her mouth.

He continued, "Roaches are creatures of darkness, thriving in places where there is neglect and chaos, much like how demonic forces are believed to inhabit spiritually corrupt environments."

Emmanuel watched as Josephine placed her other hand over her stomach. Emmanuel imagined the weight of his words moving through her intestines like a lead balloon. "How did this happen?" she asked.

"I don't know exactly, but this sort of thing doesn't happen on its own," Emmanuel replied. "*It was invited.*" A flurry of questions remained: *Who invited it? By what means was it invited? When? And for what purpose?*

One thing he knew for sure was that demonic activity followed a clear pattern of events, which he needed Josephine to understand. He took a deep breath as he settled on where to begin. "There are five stages to demonic activity. It starts with an invitation, also known as permission or encroachment, then progresses to infestation, oppression, possession, and finally... Death."

The color drained from Josephine's cheeks, leaving her already pale complexion ghostly. Her forehead wrinkled with anguish and disbelief, as if unable to digest the magnitude of Emmanuel's words.

Emmanuel knew it would be a lot for anyone to take in. He opened his notebook, prepared to walk her through each of the stages. "I listed the five stages here," he said. He read from his notes:

"Stages of Demonic Activity: 1. Invitation, 2. Infestation, 3. Oppression, 4. Possession, 5. Death."

"Oh boy," Josephine said, her eyes fixed on the notebook. "Start at the beginning."

"It was invited—given permission to be here, communicated with, or summoned somehow," he explained. "The invitation could have been direct or implied."

"Direct or implied? What's the difference?"

"It was given a direct invitation, meaning it was directly summoned through the occult—Ouija board, spells, curses..." He imagined the vacant home being occupied by squatters or ignorant thrill-seeking teenagers toying with dark forces on Halloween night, given the house's proximity to the cemetery. *Naive kids have no idea what they're toying with when they play with these things,* he thought. *I sure didn't.* "No telling what's happened in this house in the past fifty years."

"So what's an implied invitation?"

"Invited indirectly—by temptation, for example."

She shook her head. "I still don't understand."

He thought back to how he reconciled the information when he first learned it years ago. "Think of it this way," he said. "A demon will come if you call." He brought his hand to his ear and pressed his thumb to his temple as if speaking into a phone.

"Through a spirit board, spell, or curse," Josephine said. She locked eyes with Emmanuel as though struck by a realization. "What if Madeline and the girls she wrote about in the diary used a spirit board in the house? They lit candles. Madeline said they were scared."

"Anything is possible," he said. "But demons can also gain entry by simply knocking on the front door and tricking someone into letting them in, usually by offering something they know the person wants. Think of it like a child predator baiting their victim." This was the type of invitation that Emmanuel was more concerned about, given the children in the house and demons' propensity to manipulate the young and vulnerable.

"So if a child falls for the trick by taking the bait, the invitation is implied."

He nodded, "Exactly." He suddenly noticed the color drain from his wife's face. "What is it?"

"Maybe Candy took the bait," she said with wide eyes.

He shrugged his shoulders. "It's possible," he said, maintaining his gaze on her. He sensed there was more to her concern. "There's more, isn't there?"

She nodded slowly. "Emma said the little girl asked her if she wanted to be her friend," she said, swallowing hard. "Was that an invitation?"

"What little girl?" he said, his expression a mix of anger and confusion.

"Emma said she saw a little girl in the house. She said the girl asked to be her friend."

Emmanuel's eyes widened. It was the first he'd heard of this. "What did Emma say?"

"She said no. She definitely said no. She even demanded the girl leave."

He rolled his eyes skyward. "I wish you'd tell me these things." He shook his head. "I wish she'd tell me these things."

"Why is Emma the only one seeing these things, anyway? Does she have the gift of discerning spirits?"

"Demons prefer to go unseen, to remain undetected while wreaking havoc, but they have a way of revealing themselves to the young." Emmanuel saw the worry etched across her face. The creases in her forehead ran deep. He understood this was a lot for her to take in and knew she only wanted the same thing he did—to protect their daughter, their family. "The gift of discerning spirits is rare—in all likelihood, she will outgrow what she is able to see."

She nodded slowly. "OK, tell me about the next stage."

"Infestation," he said. "The demons are among us—co-existing with us in the house."

"Can they hurt us?"

"No. They cannot hurt believers. The demons may be in the house, but the people in it—we belong to God."

"In that case, why bother?"

"They want to evoke fear and push their limits. So they rebel and control whatever they can—the banging, the wall heater—all because they cannot control, possess, what they want the most: us." His own words made his heart race with fury; his chest tightened with each rapid beat.

The thought of demons being in their home. Toying with their things. Trying to manipulate their little girl. *The cowards!*

With a burst of fury, he propelled his clenched fist down, stopping just short of pounding the surface of the kitchen table. He squeezed his eyes shut and took a deep breath, forcing himself to swallow the anger that was simmering in his soul.

"I know it isn't easy, but we must resist dark emotions," Emmanuel said. "Anger, fear, anxiety, depression... These are all a part of the third stage—oppression. The demon seeks control of the mind because demons are mischievous, and the devil seeks to devour believers by scheming, using our own thoughts against us."

She nodded. "I understand."

"After oppression comes the fourth stage, possession. The demon invades the body, bringing it closer to what it's really after—the soul."

"Enter stage five," Josephine said.

EMMANUEL SENSED THEY WERE dealing with an intelligent spirit, not residual energy. The way the glass flew out of his hand at the precise time he was talking about the demon—it was no coincidence. "A portal must have been opened." Without another word, he rose to his feet and strode out of the kitchen, his steps long and purposeful.

"What are you doing?" Josephine asked, rushing to keep up.

"Searching David's room," he said, not bothering to ask for permission or give it a second thought. Privacy was a luxury they couldn't afford when evil forces were involved. They tore through the room, pulling drawers from the dresser, flipping the mattress, leaving no corner untouched.

"How will we know if we've found it?" Josephine asked, rummaging through a pile of clothes on the floor.

"A spirit board, or any evidence of witchcraft: black magic, spells, curses." Emmanuel's eyes landed on a black and red cardboard box. Strange. David hadn't mentioned having checkers, and given how close he and Emma were becoming, it seemed odd that he wouldn't have asked her to play. He pried open the lid, and there it was—the board he knew as a gateway to hell. "A Ouija board." He stared at it, disgusted by the deceptively harmless-looking game that had been linked to so much darkness. It was said to be so sinister that it was responsible for the untimely death of William Fuld, the owner of the Ouija board company, in 1927. The story went that the Ouija board had allegedly recommended that Fuld build a particular factory to expand production. While walking on the roof of this factory, Fuld leaned on a support that gave way, causing him to lose his balance and plunge to his death.

Emmanuel's glare drilled into the board, his hatred for it palpable. "What are we going to do with it?" Josephine asked, her voice trembling slightly.

Emmanuel ripped the board from the box, his grip tight, his expression fierce. "We burn it... Right now. Let's go."

They stepped out of the room and into the backyard, their steps hurried and filled with purpose. Emmanuel grabbed a shovel leaning against the house and marched to the far end of the yard. "I need you to do exactly as I say," he said, driving the shovel into the ground. "Do you understand?"

"Yes," Josephine replied, her voice steady.

"It's not enough for us to burn it," he said.

"We bury it?"

He dropped the shovel to the ground, beads of sweat forming on his brow. "First, we anoint it." He pulled a small glass bottle from his pocket, twisted the cap off, and poured the anointing oil over the board. "Now we pray."

Josephine nodded and bowed her head.

"Satan, you have no power over us. You have no power over this home,"
Emmanuel declared, his voice firm and resolute. He retrieved a lighter from his
pocket. "We are children of God, and we bind you from this home and everyone
in it!" There was a sharp click as he flicked the lighter, igniting a flame. "In the
name of the Father, the Son, and the Holy Ghost." With a swift motion, he
brought the flame to the board, releasing it from his grip and dropping it into the
freshly dug hole. They stepped back, watching as the board erupted in flames,
the fire consuming it with a fierce intensity.

The flames crackled and roared, the darkness of the night illuminated by their
light. As the board burned, a sense of finality washed over them. But deep down,
Emmanuel knew this was just the beginning.

Reflection

Maybe it was pastoral instinct. Or maybe it was the spiritual discernment forged
over decades of standing between people and principalities. But my father knew
something had shifted.

And when the unease grew too strong to ignore, he acted. He and my mother
tore through my brother's room—searching, praying, confronting. And when
he found what had been hidden—the Ouija board tucked deep beneath a pile
of old clothes—my brother says he heard it.

Not a feeling.

Not a guess.

A voice. A clear, chilling whisper that stopped him in his tracks: *He found it.*

Scripture is clear that we are not to seek guidance from spirits, mediums, or
any form of occult practice. A Ouija board might seem like a game, but it opens
the door to spiritual realms that God has warned us to stay away from.

> "There shall not be found among you anyone who burns his son
> or his daughter as an offering, anyone who practices divination
> or tells fortunes or interprets omens, or a sorcerer or a charmer
> or a medium or a necromancer or one who inquires of the

dead,

for whoever does these things is an abomination to the LORD.
"

Deuteronomy 18:10-12 (ESV)

If you're curious, scared, or tempted—know this: God is not angry at your questions. He wants you to bring them to Him. He is a loving Father who answers with truth and peace, not fear or confusion.

> "If any of you lacks wisdom, let him ask God, who gives gener-
> ously to all without reproach, and it will be given him."
>
> James 1:5 (NIV)

That season of our lives marked a turning point. It was a sobering, visceral reminder that the enemy doesn't need a wide-open door. Just a crack. A whisper. A sliver of curiosity wrapped in something that feels harmless. That's how it entered our home. And that's how it tries to enter so many others.

I'd love to say my brother never touched a spirit board again. But he did. More than once. Sometimes deliverance isn't instant—it's a process. But with age came spiritual maturity. His eyes opened. And today, he doesn't dabble. He won't even entertain it. Because he no longer just knows better—he believes better.

We often think growing up in a Christian home is a kind of spiritual shield. But what I've learned is this: where faith is real, the enemy fights harder. Where prayer is fervent, he pushes back. And where the Spirit is present, darkness lurks close by, hoping for just one invitation.

But deliverance doesn't come through fear. It comes through discernment. It comes when someone stands in the gap. My father did that for my brother. He walked into that room, not just as a protective parent, but as a spiritual warrior. He searched, found, and confronted what had been hiding. And the moment he did, something broke.

That whisper—"He found it"—wasn't just a threat. It was also a confession. Because what is found can be cast out. What is hidden can be brought to light. And what is broken can be restored.

That moment could have marked a downfall. Instead, it became a declaration. A line in the sand. A reminder that our home was holy ground—and the enemy didn't belong, even when it was invited in.

So to every parent, every guardian, every believer reading this: Watch closely. Don't ignore the shift in mood, the unexplained darkness, the sudden silence in your child's eyes. Anoint your home. Pray out loud. Speak the name of Jesus boldly. Because evil doesn't wait for permission—it waits for opportunity.

Let this story serve both as a warning... and as a promise: *The enemy may come. But he doesn't get to stay.*

Chapter 6

The Summoned

W hat happened in the house I was raised in and the things I experienced since then awakened something in me—an awareness, a sensitivity, a lifelong understanding that the veil between the physical and the spiritual is far thinner than most people realize. But while that encounter made me more cautious and spiritually alert, not everyone in my life walked away with the same sense of reverence.

I heard the warnings often growing up—not as superstition, but as spiritual truth. In our home, spiritual warfare wasn't reserved for sermons or Bible studies. It was part of our lived experience.

My father didn't just preach about it—he lived it. He had seen too much not to believe. He knew, firsthand, how the enemy disguises itself, how darkness lingers in places you'd least expect, and how the line between curiosity and danger is often thinner than we think. He would often say, "The devil doesn't need an open door—just a cracked window."

That image stayed with me. Evil doesn't always burst in. Sometimes it waits. Quiet. Familiar. Harmless-seeming. It enters through disbelief, distraction, or unchecked curiosity. And once it gains access, it does not leave without a fight.

But not everyone took those warnings seriously. Not everyone understands the stakes. The excerpt you are about to read is based on a real event that happened to someone I'll call "Melanie." Always the rebel. She sat through the same sermons I did, listened to the same stories, sang the same hymns. But where

I leaned into caution, she leaned into defiance. She liked to press against the boundaries of belief—testing the edges, laughing at the rules.

To her, the supernatural wasn't something sacred or dangerous. It was thrilling. Entertaining. A dare. She believed she was in control. That she could dabble, step back, and walk away untouched.

But what she didn't realize—and what so many fail to understand—is that once you open a spiritual door, you don't always get to choose what walks through it. And even more dangerously, you don't always get to decide when—or if—it leaves.

An Excerpt from *Infestation*

EMMANUEL RECALLED THE DETAILS of that night vividly, even after so many years.

He had been at his tía's house when he and his cousins, Jesse and Lucy, decided to toy with the spirit world. He was eleven years old, his cousins twelve and fourteen, and they were bored, searching for something to do while their mothers prepared tamales for Christmas that evening. They made a makeshift spirit board using cut-out letters from an old magazine, glue, and a piece of cardboard. Lucy and Jesse began the ritual, sitting around the coffee table and inviting a spirit to join them, using a glass as a planchette, while Emmanuel and his younger sister, Margie, observed from the couch.

"Are you sure you know what you're doing?" Emmanuel asked, a note of apprehension in his voice.

"How hard could it be?" Jesse replied with a shrug. "If there is a spirit out there, please come to my house," he said, holding the glass over the board.

"You're inviting it here?" Emmanuel said, his tone incredulous.

"I don't mean literally," Jesse replied, rolling his eyes. "I just want it to talk to us."

To their shock, the spirit revealed itself through the board, spelling out its name: Damien.

"Manny, are you going to play or not?' Lucy asked, her voice tinged with impatience.

"I want to play," Margie said, her eyes wide with curiosity.

"No! You're too young!" Emmanuel exclaimed, a protective instinct kicking in. Even then, he sensed something wicked about the board, something he needed to shield his little sister from. "I'll do it," he said, rising to his feet.

He stepped up to the table, his heart pounding with a mix of fear and doubt about whether their homemade creation would actually work. He reached for the glass, and as soon as his fingers made contact with it, the glass shot across the board with terrifying force, smashing violently against the far wall.

Their eyes were glued to the spot, their faces etched with horror and disbelief, hearts racing as they struggled to comprehend what had just happened.

"What is wrong with you, man?!" Jesse exclaimed, his voice shaking.

"I didn't do it!" Emmanuel fired back, his voice rising with fear. It was the scariest thing he had ever experienced, and every fiber of his being wanted to stop there, but he couldn't convince his cousins that he hadn't thrown the glass. "Come on, Margie, let's go," he said, grabbing her hand and dragging her out of the room.

His cousins, undeterred, continued without him. Later that evening, Emmanuel's mother received a frantic call from her sister, demanding to know what they had done and what he had seen that night. She explained that after Emmanuel and Margie had left, the kids began screaming uncontrollably, hysterical with fear, forcing her to drive them to the first Catholic church that would take her call.

She handed the phone to the priest, who asked Emmanuel to explain what had happened. Emmanuel recounted how he had stopped playing after the glass hit the wall. But he would later learn that this was only the beginning. His cousins had continued to invite the spirit and taunted its presence. He was told that every piece of glass in the house shattered that day—picture frames, windows, lightbulbs, mirrors—all reduced to shards. In a desperate attempt to end the torment, they tore the board into pieces, but to their horror, the pieces mysteriously reassembled themselves.

"My primos were never quite the same after that night," Emmanuel said, his voice heavy with the weight of the memory. But there was something else that happened, something Emmanuel had never told a soul. "I remember feeling this lingering heaviness in my chest, like I couldn't breathe. It started the moment the glass hit the wall," he began, his eyes distant, lost in the past. "Then suddenly, I saw this bright light—warm, glowing—and a woman."

"Your guardian angel?" Josephine asked, her tone a mix of curiosity and disbelief.

"I believe so," he said, his voice tinged with awe. "She had her arms extended in front of her like she was pushing something back. She said, 'Leave, he's not yours.' And then, just like that, the heaviness in my chest was gone."

He shook his head, still grappling with the significance of the moment. "We opened a portal that night. Maybe it was I who set the demon off—caused the glass to fly. Maybe it recognized me, knew who I was—who I would one day become," Emmanuel said, his voice dropping to a near whisper. "Maybe it's been watching, waiting, all along."

Reflection

Spirit boards don't connect you to God. They connect you to something far more dangerous—and far less trustworthy. And being raised in a faith-filled home doesn't make you immune to evil.

Satan doesn't waste time on those already walking in darkness. He's after the ones marked by light. And that light burns brightest in households where the Word is spoken, where worship is real, and where truth is taught. But even those homes can become battlegrounds if discernment fades or curiosity goes unchecked.

I was warned. And now, so are you.

The danger of a spirit board isn't just in what people think they're doing—it's in what they're actually inviting. Scripture teaches that we are in the middle of a spiritual battle (Ephesians 6:12), and not every spirit is friendly or harmless.

"For we do not wrestle against flesh and blood, but against the rulers, against the authorities, against the cosmic powers over this present darkness, against the spiritual forces of evil in the heavenly places."

Ephesians 6:12 (ESV)

What may seem like an innocent attempt to "talk to spirits" can actually expose someone to demonic influence or deception.

"And no wonder, for Satan himself masquerades as an angel of light."

2 Corinthians 11:14 (NIV)

The enemy is cunning—he often doesn't show up with horns and fire. He comes subtly, wrapped in curiosity or disguised as comfort. But his goal is always the same: to deceive, distract, and ultimately destroy. Christians are called to seek truth, comfort, and guidance from God alone.

We have access to the Creator of the universe through prayer, Scripture, and the Holy Spirit. We don't need to turn to unknown spirits or supernatural tools. And we're not meant to.

Don't play with spirit boards. Don't open doors you can't close. Don't give the devil a foothold.

My father didn't just preach these things from the pulpit—he carried them like armor, threading them into every conversation, every whispered prayer, every doorway he crossed. His warnings weren't rooted in superstition or fear-mongering. They were forged in fire—shaped by encounters that would shatter most people's understanding of the world. He had seen things others couldn't begin to imagine.

And because of that, he spoke with urgency, not out of arrogance, but from hard-earned wisdom. He knew how easily curiosity could become a curse. How innocent questions and casual dabbling could open doors better left sealed.

But like many truths passed down in faith-filled homes, his words were often dismissed—brushed off as dramatic, outdated, even paranoid.

That is, until you experience it for yourself. Until something steps out of the shadows and stares back at you.

What happened that day wasn't just a child's imagination or a game gone too far. It was a spiritual collision—an unseen war erupting in the most ordinary of places. One born from ignorance, rebellion, and a subtle invitation we didn't even know we had extended. It was the result of a culture that flirts with the demonic, glamorizes fear, and calls it entertainment—all while pretending there's nothing to be afraid of.

But the enemy knows better... It knew who was in that room. It recognized the opening. It saw the vulnerability, the fracture in the spiritual defenses, and it took full advantage. It didn't knock. It didn't ask. It came in, uninvited—but welcomed just the same. The glass flying across the room was only the beginning.

What followed—shattered windows, picture frames reduced to shards, mirrors exploding, and a board that reassembled itself—wasn't a haunting. It was a breach. A tearing of the spiritual barrier that once protected that space.

They were young. They didn't understand.

But the spirit world doesn't wait for understanding. It responds to permission. So, to every reader: please don't invite in what you don't understand. Don't play with the unseen as if it's entertainment. There are forces in this world that are ancient, intelligent, and hungry for influence—and they are waiting to be welcomed.

The good news?

We don't have to go searching for truth in the shadows. We don't need to summon spirits to find answers. We have a Savior who already holds all truth. And we don't have to fear what's hidden.

Because the One who is in us is greater than the one who prowls in darkness. We don't need to conjure. We just need to call on His name.

PART II

A quaint Chicago church transforms into a battleground of unspeakable horrors. The arrival of Oscar—a seemingly whimsical puppet with a tuft of fiery red hair and an unsettling, stitched-on smile—marks the beginning of a nightmare. Friends Emma and Brianna sense the malevolence beneath Oscar's cheerful facade and must confront the sinister puppet that has infiltrated her father's church and stop it before it consumes her family and the children of their congregation.

Chapter 7

The Targeted

As with each of my novels, the story behind *Oscar* was born of raw emotion. But this one is different. This story does not spring merely from imagination or secondhand accounts—it rises from the hidden recesses of my own childhood, from a memory so strange and unnerving that it lingers with me still.

What began as something outwardly innocent became the source of profound, unexplainable fear. My father, who was deeply rooted in his calling, somehow acquired a hand puppet named Oscar. To this day, he barely remembers its existence—let alone where it came from.

Oscar was peculiar.

Red, wispy hair framed the face of a boy, though the proportions were all wrong. His eyes were too wide, hollow and unblinking. His mouth curved into a smile that never shifted—too fixed, too knowing. He wore a black-and-white striped sweater and blue pants, clothes meant to appear ordinary but instead lending him an uncanny quality. In the beginning, he was meant to be a tool of ministry, a harmless prop to engage children. But for me, Oscar became something else entirely.

In the novel, something unusual—a toad—shows up at church the very day Oscar appears. The choice isn't arbitrary. Frogs appear in Scripture, most famously in the book of Exodus, when God unleashed a plague of frogs upon Egypt. They poured out of the Nile, invading homes, bedrooms, even ovens and kneading troughs. What seemed small and insignificant multiplied into suffocating judgment—a sign that what had once been tolerated had now become unbearable.

Toads, however, have carried a darker weight in folklore and spiritual traditions. Unlike frogs, which appear in the Bible as a plague of judgment, toads are often tied to witchcraft, curses, and demonic presence. Across centuries, they've been branded as carriers of poison, corruption, and deception—creatures whispered about in hushed tones, their presence considered an omen that something spiritually foul had taken root.

By pairing these threads together, the symbolism becomes undeniable: frogs in Scripture signal oppression on a massive scale, while toads in folklore point to something more personal, intimate, and insidious—like a curse crawling right to your doorstep.

And though the fiction diverges from reality, its foundation is true—based on a warning I heard time and time again growing up, a warning I still heed to this day: beware of the toad.

An Excerpt from *Oscar*

EMMANUEL HAD DISCOVERED THE TOAD the same day Oscar showed up. The realization coiled in his gut like a tightening knot, but even as the weight of it settled over him, he wasn't willing to accept the blame alone. His gaze snapped to Emma, frustration crackling through his voice. "And you didn't think finding the toad was important enough to tell me? So what? You just hid it?" His voice rose, sharp and accusatory, the tension that had been simmering now boiling over. "We've talked about this! You must have known its significance!"

Silence.

Emma didn't flinch. Arms crossed, she didn't even look at him.

"Emma." His voice was sharper now, cutting through the quiet like a blade. "Why didn't you tell me?"

Emma exhaled slowly, her hands stilling for the first time. When she finally spoke, her tone was eerily calm, drained of emotion. "Because I knew you'd think I had something to do with it." She didn't say it with anger or defiance. She said it like it was the inevitable truth. Like she had already accepted his disappointment long before this moment.

She wasn't wrong. Emmanuel inhaled sharply, gripping the steering wheel, his gaze flicking toward her before settling back on the road. "Well, did you?" His voice was quieter this time, but just as cutting.

Her head snapped toward him, eyes flashing with a mix of hurt and fury. "Of course not! I had nothing to do with it!" The words burst from her, loud and defiant, but they barely had time to settle before she caught the weight of his unwavering glare.

Her confidence wavered. She swallowed hard; her breath unsteady. "I mea n... no." This time, the word came softer, almost unsure, her voice no longer armor but something far more fragile.

"Why didn't you tell me?" he repeated.

"I knew what it would look like," she replied. "I thought you'd think I'd planted it there or that it was some kind of message I was sending. And I didn't... I don't know, Dad. I didn't know what to do or how to tell you without picturing you blaming me for the situation."

Again, she wasn't wrong. He had doubted her, if only in the fleeting, panicked recesses of his mind. The realization weighed heavily on him, a sharp pang of regret stabbing through his chest. It seemed the very respect he had hoped to instill in Emma had backfired, silencing her when he needed her honesty most.

Emma turned to face him fully, her expression raw with emotion. "What have I ever done, Dad? What have I ever done for you to think I'd be responsible for something like that? To force me to work with that *thing*? To make you think I'm a liar?"

Her words struck him hard, cutting through his defenses like a blade. He opened his mouth to respond, but the weight of her pain rendered him silent, his breath hitching in his chest. She was right—Emma had never given him a reason to doubt her. Not once. And yet, he had let his own fears cloud his trust in her.

For a moment, he stared at the road ahead, the dark horizon stretching endlessly before them. He exhaled slowly, forcing himself to speak, though the words felt sharp and jagged in his throat. He took a deep breath, pushing past the instinct to deflect, to downplay the issue, and forcing himself to confront it head-on.

"I'm sorry," he said finally, his voice low, heavy with the weight of his regret. "You're right. I should have trusted you. I should've listened to you. I should have made you feel safe—like you can tell me anything," he said. "I know I'm hard on you. And this isn't an excuse, but I'm just trying to protect you from things I can't even begin to explain. Things I can barely reconcile myself."

He paused, his fingers gripping the wheel tighter as he fought against the rising tide of guilt.

"I suppose... it's easier to attack you, to blame you, than it is to face the darkness of this world head-on. To face how powerless I sometimes feel against it."

Reflection

It is widely believed that darkness always opposes light—spiritually, morally, and even metaphorically. Darkness doesn't waste its energy on those already stumbling in shadows. Lukewarm or indifferent faith rarely stirs much opposition. But when someone carries true light—living with integrity, prayer, discernment, and faith—they shine in ways that expose deception and disrupt the enemy's plans. And when that light is revealed, it inevitably becomes a target.

That was certainly my experience growing up. I remember strategically placed items—objects heavy with meaning—left at the footsteps of our church, and even on the porch of my own home. Their purpose was never innocent. They were designed to *weaken faith, to plant seeds of fear, doubt, and despair, and to silence testimony.* Much like the excerpt you just read, where Emma concealed the truth about the toad, fear thrives in secrecy. It teaches you to bury what should be spoken aloud.

As a child, I was timid—a rule-follower terrified of getting into trouble. And so, I kept quiet. I silenced myself in ways I now pray my own children never feel they must...

But that is precisely what darkness does.

If a believer is bold about God, the enemy's strategy is to shut them up. If faith unites a community, the enemy's aim is to sow division—between families, within friendships, and even in churches. If a person knows their purpose, the enemy's tactic is distraction.

Yet, the story never ends there. Even though believers are targeted, the unshakable truth of the Christian faith is this: *light is stronger than darkness.* The attacks may be real, and they may take many forms, but they are limited. *They are temporary.* And they are always subject to the higher authority of God.

Scripture reminds us:

> "The light shines in the darkness, and the darkness has not overcome it."
>
> John 1:5 (ESV)

It also tells us:

> " No, in all these things we are more than conquerors through him who loved us."
>
> Romans 8:37 (ESV)

This is the anchor I hold to now. *What once silenced me no longer has power.* The same light that drew attack is the light that now carries authority, and that light is Christ.

Chapter 8

The Shunned

I've come to believe one of the enemy's most insidious tactics is not smoke and shadows, but shunning. The war doesn't always announce itself with spectacle—it often arrives in whispers of rejection, in the turning of familiar faces, in silence where there should have been love. The enemy knows isolation wounds deeply. When a believer is cut off from family or community, the pain can sink into the soul, causing them to question their worth, their voice, even their calling.

I learned this lesson when I was in high school. A distant relative—someone I once laughed with, shared secrets with, sat beside her at lunch every day—suddenly wanted nothing to do with me. One day we were inseparable; the next, I was invisible. Why? Because my mother had invited her mom to church.

I don't know exactly how my mother worded the invitation—what she said, what tone she used. What I do know is that an invitation meant to bring life and hope was taken as an offense, and I was guilty by association.

The fracture that followed was sharp and lasting. That wound lingers because rejection strikes at something deeper than circumstance—it strikes at identity. It isolates, silences, and feeds the lie that you are unworthy of love or connection. And often, it isn't because of what you've done, but because of what you carry.

I was too young to make sense of it, but I felt it in my bones. The sting of rejection. The shift in the air when I walked into a room. The awkward silences where laughter used to be. I hadn't done anything wrong, yet I carried the weight of being unwanted.

That's how shunning works—it turns love into distance and belonging into exile, leaving behind questions that gnaw at the spirit. *What did I do? Why am I no longer enough?* The excerpt that follows is inspired by that very experience.

An Excerpt from *Oscar*

The soft creak of the floorboards betrayed Diane's footsteps as she stepped into the living room. The stillness pressed down like a weight, thick and suffocating, as though something unseen lingered in the air.

"Yes? What is it?" she asked, her voice clipped and controlled. But beneath the composure, a flicker of unease broke through.

Byron stood in the center of the room, his stance rigid, his gaze fixed on Brianna. "It seems Brianna and Nadia had a falling out." His tone was even, but there was an edge beneath it—sharp, deliberate.

"Since when?" Diane's eyes darted between them, searching for an answer she wasn't sure she wanted to hear.

Brianna lifted a shoulder in a casual shrug, but the cracks showed—the tremor in her fingers, the evasive flick of her gaze, the hesitation in her voice. "Last week. Before winter break."

Diane's stomach clenched. How had she missed this? Brianna, Nadia, and Emma had been inseparable all year. And yet, this fracture had slipped past her without a trace.

She lowered herself to her daughter's eye level, softening her tone though the worry still threaded her words. "Sweetie, are you okay? You can tell me if something's wrong."

Brianna hesitated—only for a second. Then her eyes flicked toward Byron. Just a glance. But Diane caught it. Felt it like a splinter burrowing deep into her chest. Suspicion unfurled inside her, slow and cold.

Byron tilted his head, his voice calm but cutting. "Diane," he said carefully, "I wondered if you might have had anything to do with it." Diane recoiled, scoffing. "Me? Are you serious?" Disbelief sharpened her tone as her body stiffened, every muscle bracing against the accusation. She shook her head hard, as if she could physically cast it off. "I barely even spoke to her. She was quiet—but that's normal, isn't it? I figured she'd open up over time." A sharp breath escaped her, equal parts anger and defense. "Where is this coming from? Why would you even say that?"

Silence followed, heavy and suffocating, like the air itself was waiting.

"You've got to be kidding!" Diane snapped, her voice cutting through the stillness like glass shattering. "I have nothing against that girl!"

Her eyes swung toward Byron, expecting him to back her up, to offer the reassurance she craved. But he only stood there, measured, unreadable. Silent.

Her frustration ignited into something hotter, almost desperate. "Why would I invite Nadia's mother to church if I had an issue with—"

The words strangled in her throat. A memory surfaced—sudden, unbidden, sharp. It hit with such force her hand flew to her mouth, as if to hold it back.

Her chest tightened. The realization stabbed deep.

Byron's slow nod felt like a verdict. His voice was low, deliberate. "Mmm-hmm. I thought Nadia's mom looked a bit... unsettled when I walked up to you two that evening."

Diane's blood drained cold. She had met Nadia's mother only once. Briefly. So briefly she hadn't even remembered the woman's name. She had been eager then—too eager—to make an impression, to celebrate Brianna's new friendship.

Maybe... too eager.

"I spoke to Nadia's mother. I invited her to church," Diane admitted, collapsing onto the couch, her body sagging with the weight of realization. "She declined."

"Did you say anything else?" Brianna's voice was careful.

Diane hesitated, twisting the dishtowel in her hands. "I didn't let up." She admitted it in a rush. The words tumbled out. She remembered her own enthusiasm, how insistent she must have sounded. "I told her it could be life-changing."

Brianna exhaled sharply. "Mom, that sounds really pushy."

"I realize that now," she said. "I thought it was no different from when Emma's mom invited me to church all those years ago." But even as she spoke, regret tinged her words.

Byron's voice cut through the moment. "It was raining that day," he said. "She was soaked when I saw her standing outside."

Diane nodded. "And it was freezing. She was shivering, dripping wet. And I... I didn't even invite her in before I brought up church."

Brianna's expression darkened. "You invited her to church before asking her inside?"

Diane flinched. She heard the disbelief in Brianna's voice, felt the weight of the question settle over her like a stone.

"Before I even asked her for her name," she admitted, shame curling in her stomach. "Even then, I pushed."

Byron exhaled through his nose, contemplative. "That must've been when I walked up."

Diane nodded again, her hands limp in her lap. "It's not like me," she murmured, more to herself than anyone else.

"No," Brianna agreed, her voice firm but troubled. "It isn't." She studied her mother, confusion clouding her eyes. "Mom... what were you thinking?"

Diane closed her eyes for a moment, forcing herself to relive that evening—the sharp trill of the doorbell cutting through the kitchen, her hands slick with oil as she rushed to finish dinner before her hospital shift. She hadn't planned to invite Nadia's mother to church that evening. The thought hadn't even crossed her mind—until she opened the door.

"I... I was so caught off guard," Diane murmured, her gaze unfocused, her voice brittle with something unspoken.

"By what?" Brianna pressed, leaning in.

Diane's eyes darkened, her voice dropping to a near-whisper. "By the necklace she was wearing."

She could see it as clearly as if it were dangling before her now—a delicate gold pendant, its surface engraved with a phoenix rising from the flames. It had gleamed under the porch light, beautiful, unassuming. But then she'd reached out, instinctively, to hug the woman. And she had recoiled.

Diane's breath hitched. "She pulled back, almost like she was afraid to touch me. Her necklace flipped over, and I saw the other side of it."

Byron leaned forward, his expression taut. "What was on the other side?"

"A pentagram." Her voice barely made it past her lips. "An *inverted* pentagram."

The silence that followed pressed down on them like a suffocating fog, thick and unyielding. Diane slumped onto the couch, her hands covering her face, her shoulders bowed beneath an invisible weight. Shame? Fear? Guilt? She couldn't name it anymore. All she knew was that in that moment, something inside her gave way, a hairline fracture that deepened with every breath.

Brianna's voice broke through the stillness, quiet yet laced with a resolve that cut against the heaviness in the room. "Mom, Nadia and her mother must be responsible for all this. For what's happening with me, Emma, Janie—"

"Jonah," Byron interrupted, his tone low but firm.

Brianna's head snapped toward him, her eyes wide. "What? What happened to Jonah? Is he okay?"

Byron nodded slowly, though the tight set of his jaw betrayed him. Something flickered in his eyes—dark, unreadable, a truth restrained. His silence carried more weight than words ever could.

Reflection

The excerpt you just read serves as a reminder that rejection, as painful as it is, often comes not because we are in the wrong, but because the light in us unsettles the darkness in others. When faith shines too brightly, it confronts what others would rather keep hidden. And sometimes, the easiest response for them is to turn away.

In spiritual warfare teachings, being shunned, rejected, or isolated is often described as one of the enemy's subtle but powerful tactics. Being shunned—whether by family, friends, or even church members—can create feelings of loneliness, abandonment, and discouragement, which the enemy exploits to weaken faith.

Rejection can create shame, which silences testimony. Many spiritual warfare teachers point out that when believers are mocked or shunned for their convictions, the enemy's goal is to make them doubt their worth, question their calling, or keep them from boldly sharing the truth.

At the same time, spiritual warfare emphasizes that rejection is not just an attack—it can also be a tool of refinement. Many preachers say God allows rejection to prune believers, to strengthen dependence on Him rather than on human approval. Being shunned often pushes believers to develop deeper prayer lives, sharper discernment, and stronger identity in Christ.

> "Blessed are you when others revile you and persecute you and utter all kinds of evil against you falsely on my account."
>
> Matthew 5:11 (ESV)

Back then, I didn't understand why I was shunned. I only knew that something had broken, and I was left standing on the outside of a door that had once been open to me. Now, looking back, I see that the Scripture had already warned me:

> "If the world hates you, know that it has hated me before it hated you."
>
> John 15:18 (ESV)

Back then, those words were just verses I heard in church. But now they echo with lived meaning.

The rejection I felt wasn't just about me—it was about the light I carried without even realizing it. Faith unsettles darkness. Conviction rattles complacency.

Sometimes it's not your mistakes that make you a target, but your very presence, your willingness to believe, your quiet choice to stand apart. What I once thought was personal failure, I now understand as spiritual opposition. And that shift changes everything.

PART III

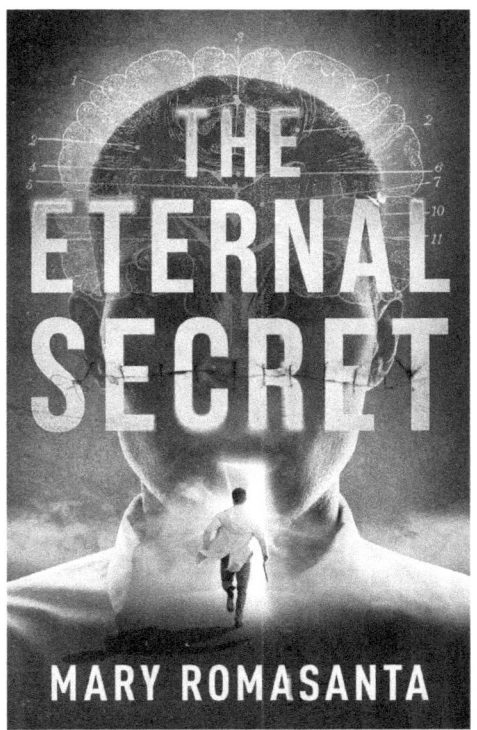

While researching near-death experiences, a brilliant neurologist uncovers a mind-bending truth: a hidden region of the brain functions as a homing device, guiding souls to the afterlife. If he can manipulate this crucial gateway before death, he may unlock the ultimate secret. But the deeper he ventures into this uncharted realm, the more he awakens forces determined to silence him—at any cost.

Chapter 9

The Dead Part I

Sometimes, faith begins where logic ends. Sometimes, it takes witnessing the inexplicable with your own eyes to finally grasp what has always been true in the spirit: we do not walk by sight—we walk by faith.

But every now and then, God allows us to see, to confirm what His Word has already declared: the unseen is just as real—if not more real—than what we can touch.

When we first met, my husband didn't believe in ghosts. To him, the supernatural was nothing more than campfire stories—entertaining, maybe, but not real. Not even my childhood encounters were enough to sway him. He listened politely, but I could tell—he thought I was exaggerating.

That changed after a trip to Boston...

It was just the two of us then, years before children. We loved exploring new cities, and part of our shared curiosity included signing up for cemetery tours. Over time, it became a tradition—not born from spiritual pursuit, but from a fascination with architecture, history, and the strange stillness of those places.

That night, the graveyard felt almost staged, like a prop from a haunted house—tilted headstones, a low mist curling at our feet, shadows cast at impossible angles. It was eerie, yes, but in a theatrical way. We left amused—entertained more than unsettled.

When we returned home, I stopped by my sister's house, as I often did after a trip, bringing souvenirs for my nieces. As I flipped through photos on my phone, casually showing her snapshots from the tour, my youngest niece leaned over my shoulder and asked a question that froze the room in place:

"Who's that man?"

I paused.

The photo she pointed to was one I'd already scrolled past countless times—just a simple picture of my husband and me, shoulder to shoulder in the cemetery, smiling in the dark.

Nothing unusual. Nothing alarming. But now, looking closer, I saw it. There, standing squarely between us, was the unmistakable figure of a man.

An apparition.

His features—hollow eyes, a sinister smile—were faint but clear enough to be human. And the more I studied the photo, the more I saw. The more I stared, the more it revealed. Shadowed faces lurking in the background. Translucent forms drifting near the graves. Layers of time folding in on themselves, captured in that single frame.

And just like that, my husband's doubt began to crumble. Since then, the novelty of cemetery tours has worn off. We still honor the dead. But now, we also honor the veil—the thin line between the living and the unseen.

That night became the seed of inspiration for the following excerpt in *The Eternal Secret*—a reminder that sometimes it takes witnessing the inexplicable for yourself to finally believe what others have known all along.

An Excerpt from *The Eternal Secret*

HE STOOD OUTSIDE THE QUAINT red brick home, the Chicago cold biting at his cheeks as he mulled over how to conduct the interview—if it could even be called that. The wind, sharp and unforgiving, seemed to cut through his coat, chilling him to the bone as his thoughts swirled like the snowflakes drifting aimlessly around him. Each flake, a fragment of a plan, dissolved as quickly as it formed, leaving him with a sense of unease.

He had anticipated more time—time to think, to plan, to rehearse how he would carefully weave Prasad's probing questions into the comforting guise of grief counseling. But Mrs. Jones had agreed to see him immediately, catching him off guard and leaving him with little more than his instincts to guide him.

Now, as he approached the door, the weight of anticipation settled over him like a heavy, invisible coat, pressing down on his shoulders, making each step feel deliberate and measured.

The red bricks of the house, dusted with a light layer of snow, stood in stark contrast to the gray sky above. The house itself was unassuming, yet as he reached for the doorbell, it felt as though he were about to cross a threshold into something far more significant than the modest exterior suggested. The door, dark wood with a brass knocker that had seen better days, loomed in front of him, a silent gatekeeper to the unknown.

His finger hovered over the button for just a moment before he pressed it, the soft chime of the bell echoing inside. *Too late to turn back now,* he thought, steeling himself for whatever awaited on the other side.

The door creaked open.

"May I help you?" A woman with curly silver hair stood in the doorway, her expression one of cautious curiosity.

"Hello, Mrs. Jones? I'm Dr. Clark," he said, his voice slightly muffled through the screen door.

"Come in, Dr. Clark," she replied, her voice quivering as she pushed the door open wider.

"Thank you for seeing me," he said, stepping inside, notebook in hand. As he crossed the threshold, he was greeted by a wave of musty air that seemed to hang in the atmosphere like a heavy curtain. The scent was familiar—he had encountered it in homes like this before, where time seemed to have stopped, leaving behind the distinct odor of age. He knew it wasn't just about getting old; the human body undergoes changes at every stage of life, each with its own scent. *But no one ever complains about the smell of a newborn baby,* he thought wryly.

"Take a seat wherever you'd like," Mrs. Jones offered, gesturing to the living room.

He stepped further in, the old wooden floors creaking beneath his feet, and lowered himself onto a worn-out couch covered in crackling plastic. "Thank you," he said as he sat, the couch groaning under his weight.

"I didn't know the hospital offered house visits," Mrs. Jones said, settling into a chair across from him.

"Yes, well, grieving is a difficult process. We want to ensure you're managing as well as you can under the circumstances," Edward replied, choosing his words carefully.

"Can I get you some water?" she offered, her hands fluttering nervously in her lap.

"No, I'm fine. Thank you," he replied, offering a gentle smile. "Please, sit—tell me how you're doing."

She lowered herself into a chair across from him, her movements slow and deliberate. "I'm fine," she said, her voice soft but steady.

Edward gazed at her through the dust particles floating in the dim light that filtered through the old curtains. "Are you getting out of the house and engaging in your normal activities and hobbies?"

Mrs. Jones tilted her head slightly, her eyes narrowing as she considered his question. "Funny you ask about getting out of the house."

"Oh?" he said, raising his brows, intrigued by the unexpected response. It was a standard question, but something in her tone suggested there was more beneath the surface.

"It's strange, but I don't feel like he's gone."

"That's quite normal," Edward replied, leaning forward slightly. "When we form strong emotional bonds with someone, their presence can remain alive in our hearts and minds."

"I know, but that isn't what I mean." She paused, taking a sip of water. "After being married so long—fifty-two years this November—I developed a sense of knowing when he wasn't home," she explained, her voice tinged with nostalgia.

"Please, elaborate," Edward encouraged.

"You know, he'd run to the corner store, go out and fetch the mail, work out back in the shed... He didn't always announce when he was leaving or going outside; he didn't need to. I could just sense when he wasn't in the house," she said, her eyes flicking around the room as if expecting to catch a glimpse of him. "The house just felt—"

"Empty?" Edward offered, his voice gentle.

"Exactly," she replied, nodding slowly. "Empty."

"I've been married for almost twenty years," Edward said, trying to connect with her on a personal level. "I think I know what you mean."

"But I never get that sense anymore—that sense that he isn't in the house," she said, her voice growing quieter. "Not that I lost it... It's just I feel like he never left, like he's always here... With me."

Edward hesitated, unsure how to proceed. "I know it's hard, but the first step in processing grief is accepting the reality of loss," he said, his words feeling inadequate.

"Reality of the loss? I've accepted the reality of the loss," she said, shaking her head firmly. "My husband had terminal brain cancer; he suffered for a very long time, and he lived much, much longer than doctors ever expected. He was ready to pass, and I was ready to let him go."

"But have you really?" Edward asked, his brow furrowing in concern. "Have you really accepted the reality of the loss, I mean?"

"The doctors and medical staff prepared us, and we had a long time—more time than we imagined—to process, make peace with it, make arrangements and what not," she said, her voice steady but tinged with lingering sorrow. "He was in so much pain. Every day he lived only prolonged his suffering."

Edward looked into her eyes, trying to read the emotions hidden there. She spoke as if she had accepted her husband's death, but the pain in her eyes suggested otherwise.

"It's been six months since he passed, is that right?" he asked, flipping through his notebook for confirmation.

There was silence. He looked up to find Mrs. Jones staring off into the distance, lost in thought.

"Mrs. Jones?" he prompted gently.

She jolted slightly, as if suddenly remembering she wasn't alone. "I'm sorry. What was the question?"

Edward set his notebook aside and leaned back in his seat, trying a different approach. "What's on your mind?"

"Do you think it's possible that my husband's spirit is still here?" she asked, her voice tinged with both curiosity and hesitation.

Edward's eyes widened slightly. Thoroughly unprepared for the question, he cleared his throat. "Well, finding an enduring connection with your loved one while embarking on a new life is an important part of the grieving process," he said, attempting to steer the conversation back to familiar ground.

"You know that's not what I mean," she said, her tone growing firmer. "What I mean is, do you think it's possible that his spirit is still here? In the house?"

Edward shifted uncomfortably in his seat, the plastic covering clinging to his skin like a barrier between him and the worn cushions beneath. "I don't know," he admitted, clearly out of his comfort zone. "That's not exactly my field of expertise."

She gazed at him with squinted eyes, as if measuring his response. "May I show you something, Dr. Clark?" she asked.

"Yes, of course," he replied, curious about what she was about to reveal.

Mrs. Jones turned to a small wooden cabinet beside the couch and opened the top drawer. "This will just take a moment," she said, rummaging through the contents. "Here it is! Look here. Tell me what you see," she said, handing him a photograph.

Edward examined the color photo, which depicted a younger Mr. and Mrs. Jones, likely in their early forties, standing with two children.

"It looks like a family vacation photo," he said, raising his brow. "Interesting setting."

She chuckled softly. "Growing up, my children loved Halloween almost as much as they loved Christmas."

"Are they yours?" Edward asked.

"Yes, they were twelve and fourteen back then," she replied, her voice tinged with fondness. "We visited Boston on vacation, and our boys convinced us to take them on one of those guided cemetery tours."

"I'm not sure I would have agreed to that," Edward said, a faint smile tugging at his lips.

"The kids showed us a brochure they picked up at our hotel—in the photos, the tour guides were all dressed up in old-timey costumes. My husband and I didn't believe in ghosts, spirits, whatever you want to call them, but it looked like it could be fun, so we figured, why not?"

"That's nice," he said, handing the photo back to her.

"Wait!" she exclaimed. "Take a closer look."

Oh, I get it, Edward thought. *She must be trying to tell me she captured a photo of a ghost. He brought the photo closer to his face.*

"I'll be honest, Mrs. Jones, I don't know what I'm look—"

He froze.

His eyes darted across the photo, quickly noticing the anomalies he had overlooked before. Two glowing green figures with child-like silhouettes hovered in the background over Mrs. Jones's shoulder. He blinked, doubting what he was seeing. *Probably just a lighting issue*, he thought, but the more he stared, the more he noticed—orbs of different sizes surrounding the family, some white, some yellow, all emitting a warm, ethereal glow.

He handed the photo back to Mrs. Jones, his mind grappling with the image that defied logical explanation.

"Did you spot the unusual fellow that smiled for the camera?" she asked, her voice a mix of curiosity and anticipation.

"The unusual fellow?" Edward repeated, his brow furrowing in confusion. "Are you referring to Mr. Jones?"

"No, of course not," she said, shaking her head. "Go ahead—have another look."

With a sigh, Edward brought the photo back to his face.

His heart skipped a beat.

There, in the moonlit background, was a ghostly figure—a fog-like presence with the distinct shape of a man. The apparition floated, ethereal and unsettling, with a thin frame and shoulder-length swirly hair that seemed to dance in an unseen breeze. The figure's features were clearly defined, with hollow eyes that appeared to peer into his very soul, their depths filled with an eerie emptiness.

The figure's gaunt cheeks hinted at a life drained of vitality, and yet it stood among the living, perfectly positioned between the Joneses' children, exuding a chilling self-awareness that seemed to acknowledge its own demise. Most unsettling of all was the haunting smile stretched across its lips, too wide, too knowing—a visceral reminder of the fragile boundary between life and death.

Edward placed the photo on the coffee table, his hands trembling slightly as he retreated into his seat. An unexplainable heaviness settled upon him, bridging the gap between disbelief and a newfound sense of uncertainty.

"You saw him, didn't you?" Mrs. Jones asked softly.

Edward nodded slowly, his mind reeling.

"Would you like some water, Dr. Clark?" she asked again, her voice gentle but concerned.

"No, thank you," Edward replied, clearing his throat, his voice betraying his unease.

"Are you sure?" she pressed, her concern deepening.

"Yes—why do you ask?" he inquired, his voice tinged with confusion.

"Because—"

She hesitated, searching for the right words.

"Well, there's really no other way to put this, now is there? You look like you've just seen a ghost."

Reflection

My husband is a man of science.

Rooted in reason, logic, and observable evidence, he has always approached the world through what could be tested, measured, replicated, and explained. When we first met—and for many years into our marriage—he believed that everything had a natural explanation. Not out of arrogance or dismissal, but because he had been trained to trust only what could be proven. Evidence mattered. Data mattered. Anything beyond that belonged, in his mind, to speculation.

That was the world he knew. And in many ways, it had served him well.

It would be far too simplistic to say that a single photograph changed his mind. That moment in Boston—the apparition captured between us in an image—was not a conversion experience. It was a catalyst. A fracture in a world-view that had once felt airtight. A crack in the door.

What truly shifted him was not the image itself, but what followed. The long conversations that stretched late into the night. The questions he could no longer dismiss so easily. The moments—quiet, undeniable, deeply personal—that began stacking on top of one another until coincidence no longer sufficed as an explanation.

Over time, through prayer, study, and lived experience, my husband began to grow spiritually. He started to see what he once would have waved away. His eyes softened. His heart opened. Not because I debated him into belief or argued him into faith, but because the Holy Spirit—patient, gentle, unwavering—revealed truth in His own way and in His own time.

And I want to be very clear here: I am not suggesting that the apparitions we witnessed—or those I have encountered—were the spirits of the dead. Scripture does not support that notion. Cemeteries, however, have long been places where rituals are performed, where spiritual boundaries are intentionally crossed, where things are summoned that should never be invited. I will go deeper into that reality in the next chapter.

What I am saying is this: we do not live in a world made solely of flesh and bone.

We live in a world of flesh and spirit.

And the more spiritually awake you become, the more clearly you begin to see how deeply intertwined the two truly are. What happens in the unseen realm often shapes what manifests in the seen. The physical is not isolated from the spiritual—it is influenced by it, pressed upon by it, and at times, confronted by it.

The enemy would prefer we ignore this. He would rather we explain away the strange, silence the spiritual, and reduce the supernatural to metaphor or fiction. But Scripture leaves no room for such denial:

> "For though we walk in the flesh, we are not waging war according to the flesh. For the weapons of our warfare are not of the flesh but have divine power to destroy strongholds. "
>
> 2 Corinthians 10:3–4 (ESV)

The veil is real. And so is the One who tore it.

Because of that truth, we no longer laugh off the supernatural. We do not reduce it to harmless curiosity, late-night speculation, or campfire entertainment. We do not flirt with it lightly or speak of it casually, as though it were something neutral or inconsequential. Experience has taught us otherwise.

We honor the reality of spiritual warfare. We understand now that reverence matters. There are realms beyond what we can see, and they are not imaginary. We have witnessed what happens when that realm collides with this one—when the unseen presses into the seen—and we know better than to dismiss it as fantasy or psychological projection.

Yet those encounters did not shake our faith.

They strengthened it.

Because now we both know this with certainty: the unseen is not a myth. It is eternal. And there are moments—rare, intentional moments—when God pulls back the curtain just enough to remind us that the world is far larger than what our eyes can perceive. That what we wrestle against is not of flesh and blood. And that we were never meant to face it alone.

When you understand who lives within you, fear loses its grip. When you know whose authority you carry, intimidation has no power. Darkness may still come against you, but it no longer defines the outcome.

Because greater is the One who dwells in you than anything that rises against you.

Chapter 10

The Dead Part I

My belief in ghosts—specifically, the spirits of the deceased—traces back to the encounter I shared at the beginning of this book, and it was reinforced by the strange and unsettling experiences that colored my upbringing.

As a child, my understanding of the unseen world was shaped not by theology, but by what I absorbed from the culture around me. Movies, whispers, and playground stories all carried the same message: ghosts were just like people. Some were good, some were bad, and like people, you simply learned to live alongside them.

It made sense to me then. Good ghosts protected. Bad ghosts haunted. There were categories, rules. They stayed in their lane, and as long as we stayed in ours, there was a fragile balance. That belief brought a strange comfort—an illusion of control in a world where the supernatural pressed too close, too often.

But as I grew older, I began to understand that the lines weren't so clear. What I thought were "good" spirits, even the seemingly harmless ones, carried an unease that lingered.

Their presence didn't bring peace; it stirred questions, fear, doubt. What I'd once accepted as innocent turned out to be something far more complicated, and far more dangerous.

In the excerpt from *The Eternal Secret* you are about to read, Emma comes face-to-face with a harsh truth. She confronts a lie she had unknowingly carried for most of her life—the belief that what she was seeing were the spirits of the departed. Her father's correction is firm yet tender, and in it, she finds a revelation that mirrored the kinds of conversations I overheard countless times growing up.

Still, even after everything I had seen with my own eyes, I wrestled with disbelief. I wanted to cling to the simpler explanation—that I was haunted by ghosts. But the truth remained, sharp and immovable: *There are no such things as ghosts.*

An Excerpt from *The Eternal Secret*

"I'VE SEEN THEM," Emma declared, her voice trembling as she locked eyes with her father. The conviction in her words was unshakable, as though her entire life depended on the truth she had always believed in. "You know I have."

Her father inhaled deeply, his face a mask of sorrow. "Mija, there is no such thing as ghosts."

The words hit Emma like a physical blow. Her eyes widened in disbelief, her mouth falling open as though she had forgotten how to speak. How could he say this? The man who had always stood by her, believed her, defended her when her mother dismissed her claims, was now denying everything.

"Dad—how could you?" she whispered, her voice cracking under the weight of betrayal. "After everything I've been through?"

Edward, who had been quietly observing, finally spoke up, his voice tinged with disbelief. "You lied to us?"

"No, of course not!" Emma blurted, her tone a mix of desperation and incredulity.

She turned back to her father, her eyes pleading. "Dad, I saw them—you know I did. I still see them. I just went with Edward to a couple of funeral homes this week, and I saw them."

Her father's expression remained firm, but there was a flicker of something—regret, perhaps?—in his eyes. "Why would you do that?" he asked, his tone laced with disappointment.

"To prove Prasad's theory. And I saw them—I proved his theory," she insisted, her voice growing louder, as if volume alone could force him to believe her.

Her father shook his head slowly. "The only thing you proved is that demons are cunning and keenly aware of our weaknesses and desires."

Emma's heart sank. "I don't understand... Dad, please help me understand," she begged, gripping his hand as if it were a lifeline.

He took a deep breath, as if preparing himself to shatter her world. "There are no such things as ghosts—only demons, very capable of appearing as the dead, as well as taking on any number of deceptive disguises for the purposes of evil."

Emma's eyes searched her father's face, hoping to find some trace of the man who had always believed her. But his expression was resolute, and her hopes began to crumble. "You didn't tell me when I was younger because you didn't want to scare me," she said, more a statement than a question, as realization dawned on her.

"And I thought there was a chance you would grow out of it," he added softly.

An unsettling silence enveloped the room, thick with the weight of unspoken fears and shattered beliefs. "I'm sorry, mija. I was wrong."

Emma's grip on her father's hand tightened as she tried to process this new reality. "That's why I always felt oppressed when I was around them. That's why I always ran the other way."

Her father nodded solemnly. "Because you felt the evil, even if you didn't know it was there."

"The gift of discerning spirits," Emma whispered, her voice tinged with awe as the pieces began to fall into place. "I get it now... it's not about seeing ghosts—it's about distinguishing spirits, good from evil." She turned to Prasad, her eyes blazing with intensity. "We shouldn't even be talking about this."

Prasad, taken aback by her sudden change in demeanor, crossed his arms. "Explain."

Emma began pacing the room, her movements sharp and rapid as she tried to articulate her thoughts. "Let's say someone is thinking about their afterlife—we all do it at some point—and they think there's a good chance they're destined for hell. Or maybe they're not even sure—maybe they think it could go either way for them. If they buy into your theory, what's to stop them from putting a bullet in their head?"

Prasad frowned, struggling to keep up with her line of reasoning. "I suppose..." he began, but Emma cut him off.

"Which means what?" she demanded.

"I don't know," Prasad admitted, his frustration growing.

"It means the poor soul that takes their own life goes to hell, while the demon that corrupted them stays in this dimension for eternity." Emma's voice was almost a growl, her fear morphing into anger.

"Absolutely," her father interjected, his voice filled with the certainty of years of experience. "And that is the larger, far more sinister issue at hand."

"An infestation of the worst kind," Emma muttered, her mind racing.

Prasad, still reeling from the rapid shift in the conversation, shook his head in confusion. "An infestation? With all due respect, darling, don't you think you're being a bit dramatic?"

"Not even close," her father countered, his voice stern. "Saint Angela Merici once said, 'Consider that the devil doesn't sleep but seeks our ruin in a thousand ways.' And the traditional prayer to Saint Michael asks for God's protection from 'Satan and all the evil spirits who prowl about the world seeking the ruin of souls.' There is no such thing as a random occurrence of bad luck. Demons manipulate everything."

Prasad stared at him, trying to wrap his mind around the implications. "How do you know all this?" he asked, his voice barely above a whisper.

"He's not only been a pastor for more than three decades," Emma said, her voice strong and clear, "but he's also performed countless exorcisms and has a Ph.D. in theology. Trust me when I say he knows a thing or two about evil."

Reflection

What Emma experiences in the story—the confusion, the revelation, the righteous anger—are emotions I've wrestled with, too. Because once you realize that what you're dealing with isn't innocent or benign, everything changes. You stop entertaining evil. You stop explaining it away. You start fighting it—with prayer, with Scripture, with the authority given to us in the name of Jesus.

The dead cannot roam the earth.

The Bible teaches that when people die, they do not remain to haunt the living. Their souls are taken to judgment, and they cannot return at will. What many interpret as "ghosts" are actually demons in disguise, exploiting human grief, fear, or curiosity.

Their goal is deception—keeping people chasing shadows instead of clinging to the truth of Christ. Luke 16:19–31 shows this in Jesus' parable: the dead are in fixed places—either comfort or torment. The rich man asks for permission to return and warn his family, but he is denied. This reveals that the dead do not return to visit the living.

Spirits that appear as the dead are deceptive.

There are spirits—some holy, some fallen. And the devil, who disguises himself as an angel of light, has no hesitation in allowing demons to masquerade as the dead if it keeps us distracted—chasing shadows instead of clinging to truth. If Satan can disguise himself in glory, demons can certainly disguise themselves as familiar loved ones to deceive and mislead.

> "And no wonder, for even Satan disguises himself as an angel of light."
>
> 2 Corinthians 11:14 (ESV)

Apparitions in Scripture were *not ghosts.*

When Jesus walked on water, the disciples thought He was a ghost—but they were wrong.

> "But when the disciples saw him walking on the sea, they were terrified, and said, 'It is a ghost!' and they cried out in fear."
>
> Matthew 14:26 (ESV)

Their fear shows that the concept of ghosts was cultural superstition, not biblical truth. And when Moses and Elijah appeared at the Transfiguration as written in the book of Matthew, they did not wander from the grave but were allowed by God to appear for His divine purpose:

> "And after six days Jesus took with him Peter and James, and John his brother, and led them up a high mountain by themselves.
> And he was transfigured before them, and his face shone like the sun, and his clothes became white as light.
> And behold, there appeared to them Moses and Elijah, talking with him."
>
> Matthew 17:1–3 (ESV)

In my story, Emma's realization mirrors something I've come to understand myself: the gift of discerning spirits isn't about seeing ghosts. It's about seeing *truth*. It's the ability to recognize what is holy and what is hostile. It's knowing the difference between a gentle nudge from the Spirit and a calculated attack from the enemy.

Discernment peers beyond appearances.

It senses the atmosphere no one else can name—the heaviness in a room, the subtle shift in tone, the unease that isn't just "in your head." It's spiritual vision, allowing you to recognize the source behind the surface. And often, it comes not to frighten us but to equip us—to remind us that while not every presence is of God, His Spirit empowers us to tell the difference and stand firm.

This isn't superstition. It's Scripture:

> "Beloved, do not believe every spirit, but test the spirits to see whether they are from God, for many false prophets have gone out into the world.
> By this you know the Spirit of God: every spirit that confesses

that Jesus Christ has come in the flesh is from God,

and every spirit that does not confess Jesus is not from God.

This is the spirit of the antichrist, which you heard was coming

and now is in the world already."

1 John 4:1-2 (ESV)

PART IV

After losing her husband and two children, a woman faces devastating tragedy. Wracked with grief and guilt, she succumbs to the siren call of despair, haunted by the ghostly legend of La Llorona—the Weeping Woman said to lure the grieving to their doom. But her daughter-in-law, a determined technologist driven by love and loss, isn't ready to let her go.

Chapter 11

The Grieving

*L*a Llorona: The Awakening is the only novel discussed in this book that is not part of what I call the *Infestation* series. I considered omitting it. The characters are different. The setting is different. The narrative stands apart from the thread that ties the other stories together.

But I could not leave it out. Because grief cannot be left out.

Though the faces change and the circumstances shift, the battle beneath the surface remains the same. *La Llorona* confronts a dimension of spiritual warfare that is quieter than what unfolds in *Infestation*, but no less dangerous. It explores what happens when loss settles into a home and lingers—when sorrow reshapes identity, distorts memory, and tempts the living to carry burdens they were never meant to bear.

To exclude this novel would have been to avoid one of the most universal and misunderstood battlefields of all.

Grief.

And grief, left unexamined, can be as spiritually consequential as any visible haunting. Not as a side note. Not as a poetic aside. But as a force.

Grief has shaped the stories I tell and the theology I carry. It shaped my childhood more than I realized at the time, and it sits at the very center of *La Llorona: The Awakening*. To ignore it here would be to speak about spiritual warfare without acknowledging one of its most vulnerable battlegrounds.

The stories that inspired *La Llorona* are different from the ones I've shared so far. They are not stories of shadows in hallways or oppressive atmospheres that pressed in without warning. They are quieter. Heavier. More human.

They are stories of absence.

The Mexican folktale of La Llorona tells of a mother who, in her despair, drowns her children and is condemned to wander the earth wailing for them. It is a story we grow up hearing as children—half warning, half myth. But beneath the folklore lies something deeper than superstition. It is a story about grief untethered from hope. Grief that curdles into madness. Grief that becomes destructive.

In *La Llorona: The Awakening*, I wove that legend together with the biblical story of Naomi and Ruth—another story marked by devastating loss. Naomi loses her husband. Then her sons. She is emptied of the future she imagined. When she returns to Bethlehem, she says, "Do not call me Naomi; call me Mara, for the Almighty has dealt very bitterly with me" (Ruth 1:20).

Two women. Two losses. Two very different outcomes.

One story ends in wandering and wailing. The other, in redemption and restoration. In that fragile state, we are vulnerable.

Grief makes us long for what we cannot have back. It makes us listen for voices that are no longer there. It makes us ache for one more word, one more touch, one more chance.

And the enemy knows this.

The excerpt you are about to read captures a different kind of haunting—not by spirits of the dead, but by memory, by regret, by love interrupted. The house Ruth enters is not possessed. It is saturated. Saturated with loss. Saturated with unfinished sentences. Saturated with the quiet despair that settles when hope feels delayed.

An Excerpt from *La Llorona: The Awakening*

Ruth's eyes darted across the living room, fingers twitching at her sides. The house felt less like shelter than a tomb—walls thick with memory, air heavy with grief. Every corner hummed with absence, pressing in on her breath.

The couch sagged in the middle, still bearing the faint imprint of nights Greg had collapsed there after long shifts. Family photos crowded the walls, their frozen smiles mocking her with the illusion of permanence. Even the floorboards groaned beneath her feet, not just with age but with echoes she could almost hear.

This wasn't a home. Not anymore.

It was a shrine. A place unwilling to let go.

A sharp crack split the stillness.

Ruth flinched, her heart vaulting into her throat. Gizmo yelped in her arms, trembling.

The bathroom pipes. The ones John said he would fix.

The noise stretched too long, too jagged, twisting into something more than faulty plumbing. A taunt. A cruel reminder of undone chores, of a life ripped mid-sentence. The water's rhythmic hum pressed at her ears like a ghost—of duty, of presence, of love severed too soon

She swallowed hard, caging the ache. She couldn't unravel now. Not here. Not again.

Footsteps cut through the quiet. Mi-Ra entered the living room, posture taut, her face unreadable, fatigue etched in every line.

"It'll only be for a couple of weeks," Ruth said, clearing her throat.

"I don't need a babysitter," Mi-Ra snapped, clipped and defensive. "And I certainly don't need you hovering over me."

"I'm not trying to babysit you," Ruth replied evenly. "My therapist thinks I should weather the storm with you."

The word storm stuck in her mouth—too simple, too poetic for something this devastating.

Mi-Ra scoffed, rolling her eyes.

Ruth thought she caught a flicker of hesitation beneath the gesture, but it was gone as quickly as it came.

"I'm fine," Mi-Ra said. Her tone carried more insistence than conviction. "Besides, where would you even sleep?"

"The couch," Ruth answered quickly. She couldn't bring herself to suggest the spare bedroom—John's old room, now cluttered with JJ's trophies and ribbons, a sports museum frozen in time.

Mi-Ra crossed her arms, glowering, skepticism etched into every hard line of her posture. But Ruth saw the cracks anyway: dishes stacked in the sink, dust collecting on once-immaculate shelves, unopened mail scattered like neglected duties across the counter. Signs that Mi-Ra wasn't fine at all.

"John would've wanted this," Ruth said quietly. She braced for resistance; pride and grief were volatile, and Mi-Ra had both in spades.

"Fine," Mi-Ra muttered, flicking her hand as though swatting away a gnat. "But not because I need you here."

Ruth nodded, letting the barb slide past. She didn't care how Mi-Ra framed it. What mattered was that she was here. Not for comfort. Not for reconciliation. Not for kindness.

She had stopped hoping for warmth from Mi-Ra years ago. That wish had suffocated under sharp looks and paper-thin civility. Approval was a ghost she no longer chased.

She wasn't here for peace.

She was here for John. For love. For loyalty. For what he had left behind. Even if that meant enduring Mi-Ra's jagged edges, grief slicing her like broken glass.

Without another word, Mi-Ra turned, her footsteps heavy on the groaning floorboards. A door clicked shut, leaving Ruth alone in the stale quiet.

She moved to the couch. It sagged beneath her, worn and lumpy, but comfort wasn't the point. She dragged a throw blanket around her shoulders. Its coarse fibers scratched her skin—another reminder that nothing in this house was soft anymore.

She lay still in the hush, her mind circling John's crooked smile, his laugh, the warmth of a family she thought would last. Each memory sharpened into ache. And the ache gave way to nothingness, so complete it hollowed her.

"Time heals all wounds," she whispered, bitterness searing her tongue. The words felt like a lie.

Her father's death had taught her the truth. Time didn't heal. It numbed. Wounds never vanished; they simply stopped screaming. Scar tissue thickened, dulling the pain, but beneath it the injury lived on—waiting for the lightest touch to tear it open again.

And grief demanded more than endurance. It demanded movement. You didn't just mourn the dead—you acted for them. You carried their wishes forward, even when they'd never spoken them aloud. You became their echo.

She had done it once before. Now John was gone. And the only way to honor him was to tend to what he'd left behind.

Even if what he left behind was Mi-Ra.

Reflection

Let me be clear: Grief is not evil. Jesus wept (John 11:35):

> "When Jesus saw her weeping, and the Jews who had come with
> her also weeping, he was deeply moved in his spirit and greatly
> troubled.
> And he said, "Where have you laid him?" They said to him,
> "Lord, come and see."
> Jesus wept. "
>
> John 11:33–35 (ESV)

The Son of God did not rebuke sorrow. He entered it. He was deeply moved. He was troubled. He stood at a graveside and wept.

Grief is the price of love in a fallen world.

But grief becomes dangerous when it is untethered from truth.

In my upbringing, I witnessed how loss could create openings—emotional fractures where questions rushed in and lingered:

Why did God allow this? Why didn't He intervene? Why does heaven feel silent?

Unanswered grief can morph into accusation. Prolonged grief can drift into despair. And despair, if left unchecked, can become agreement with lies.

This is where spiritual warfare often hides—not in horror-movie manifestations, but in quiet internal narratives:

You are alone. This will never get better. God has abandoned you. There is no future left.

Notice how subtle that shift is. Sorrow becomes interpretation. Pain becomes theology.

La Llorona wanders because she cannot move forward. Naomi, crushed by loss, nearly renames herself "Bitter." Yet Ruth chooses loyalty over isolation. Through her decision—simple, relational, covenantal—redemption enters the story.

That is not accidental.

Grief demands movement. Not forgetting. Not suppressing. But movement.

We are meant to mourn—but not to remain suspended in mourning.

Scripture never instructs us to deny sorrow. It calls us to bring it somewhere.

> "Cast your burden on the Lord, and He will sustain you; He will never permit the righteous to be moved."
>
> Psalm 55:22 (ESV)

Grief carried alone grows heavy enough to distort reality. Grief surrendered to God becomes soil for resurrection.

In *La Llorona: The Awakening*, the sound of water becomes symbolic—dripping pipes, rhythmic echoes, the suggestion of something unfinished. In folklore, water is often a place of death. In Scripture, it is also a place of rebirth: the flood that cleansed, the Red Sea that delivered, the waters of baptism that signify new life.

The enemy would like grief to drown us.

God uses it to refine us.

The difference lies in where we turn.

When Ruth chooses to remain with Mi-Ra, she is not chasing approval. She is honoring love. She is choosing covenant over comfort. That decision mirrors the biblical Ruth, who said to Naomi:

> "Do not urge me to leave you or to return from following you.
> For where you go I will go, and where you lodge I will lodge.
> Your people shall be my people, and your God my God."
>
> Ruth 1:16 (ESV)

Grief can isolate. Or it can bind people together in sacred loyalty.

It can hollow us out. Or it can make space for God to fill what we could not rebuild ourselves.

The danger is not grief itself.

The danger is hopeless grief.

And hopelessness is never from God.

> "But we do not want you to be uninformed, brothers, about those who are asleep, that you may not grieve as others do who have no hope."
>
> 1 Thessalonians 4:13 (ESV)

Notice what Paul does not say. He does not say, *do not grieve.* He says, *do not grieve without hope.*

Hope does not erase pain.

It anchors it.

Grief will visit every life.

But it does not have permission to rule it.

Chapter 12

The Lost

Loss of any kind—expected or sudden—is unbearable in its own way. Even when we anticipate it, even when illness or circumstance prepares us for what is coming, the finality still shocks the system. Death rearranges the air we breathe. It alters the atmosphere of a room. It changes how sound carries, how memory surfaces, how ordinary moments feel.

But when loss is paired with uncertainty—when there is no answer, no accountability, no explanation—the suffering deepens. The mind does not simply grieve; it spirals. Grief alone is heavy. Grief without clarity is destabilizing.

And in that instability, something subtle can happen.

The devil rarely storms in through the front door. He slips in through cracks.

Uncertainty creates cracks.

When facts are absent and questions linger, the imagination strains to fill the silence. Doubt inches closer. Anger searches for direction. The heart becomes vulnerable to narratives that feel plausible simply because they offer something solid to hold.

The forensic breakthrough described in the excerpt that follows—dog hair recovered from a suspect's clothing, matched through DNA testing—is not fictional invention. It happened. A grieving family waited for answers, suspended between hope and dread. Law enforcement pursued every fragment of evidence with painstaking care. And in the end, it was the family dog's DNA that helped identify the killer.

In *La Llorona: The Awakening*, I adapted this event into Ruth and Mi-Ra's story because grief without resolution can calcify into something dangerous. When there is no conclusion, sorrow does not settle—it hardens. It turns inward. It looks for someone, or something, to blame.

The detail itself sounds almost improbable, like something a novelist would construct to give a story symmetry—poetic justice wrapped neatly in science. But truth often carries a narrative weight that fiction struggles to replicate.

For days in real life, there were no answers. Only silence. Only theories. Only the unbearable replaying of the last known moments—conversations revisited, timelines dissected, possibilities rehearsed in the dark. And then something almost invisible—a few strands of dog hair—became the thread that unraveled the lie.

Not dramatic. Not cinematic.

Just precise. Just factual. Just enough to steady the spiral.

An Excerpt from *La Llorona: The Awakening*

The night air clung damp and cold, seeping into Mi-Ra's skin as they lingered on the driveway. The patrol car idled at the curb, its engine humming—a low, persistent warning that refused to fade.

She broke first.

"Come in," she urged, her voice pitched low and too quick. Her hand brushed the doorframe, a tentative, coaxing gesture, as if crossing the threshold might soften whatever was coming. "Please—whatever it is you need to say, you can say it in here."

Detective Gomez shook his head. His tone remained calm, measured—but the steel beneath it was unmistakable.

"No. Out here is fine."

His eyes flicked toward Paul. A dismissal. Wordless. Final.

Ruth caught it instantly. She pressed the keys into Paul's palm with quiet insistence. "Why don't you wait inside."

Paul lifted his own set, the metal glinting under the streetlight. "I'll let myself in."

Mi-Ra's brow tightened as she watched him go. The thought struck sharp and unwelcome:

Why does he still have keys to my house?

Suspicion lodged deep, cold and immovable.

The front door shut behind him with a dull, decisive thud.

Mi-Ra clasped her hands together, willing them to stop trembling. When she spoke, her voice was tight, stretched thin to the point of breaking. "Well?" She leaned toward Gomez, eyes locked on his. "What is it?"

The question carried more than curiosity. It rang like a plea—desperation wrapped in civility. She had waited too long for an answer.

Gomez didn't rush. His delivery was deliberate, each word weighed before it left his mouth.

"We recovered dog hair from the trench coat belonging to our person of interest. We believe it was transferred during a physical confrontation—most likely from your husband to the suspect."

Ruth's brow furrowed. "It's Gizmo's?"

Gomez gave a single, firm nod. "A direct DNA match. The strands were embedded deep in the lining. There's no innocent explanation for it—unless it happened during a struggle."

Mi-Ra's throat tightened. Her voice dropped, urgent and brittle. "You're absolutely certain?"

"As certain as forensics allows," he replied. His tone stayed even, but conviction burned beneath it. "The odds of two unrelated dogs sharing a complete genetic profile are less than one in several million. We're talking over 99.99 percent certainty."

Ruth exhaled, some of the tension draining from her shoulders. "So that's it? Case closed?"

Gomez's gaze didn't waver. "Technically, it's circumstantial evidence. But taken together with everything else—the suspect's shoes, the platform soles matching both the surveillance footage and the injury trajectory, plus multiple witness statements—I'd say we've got our man."

Mi-Ra swallowed hard. Relief should have rushed in, steadying her, filling the fractures grief had carved through her. Instead, a chill crept up her spine.

Proof. Certainty. Closure.

The words sounded solid in the detective's mouth, but inside her they rang hollow. Because deep down, she knew the truth—

Catching her son's killer didn't mean the nightmare was over. At least not yet.

Reflection

Resolution does not erase the loss. It does not resurrect the dead. It does not rewind the moment that shattered everything.

But it pierces the fog.

And in spiritual warfare, fog matters.

When the real-life DNA results came back, something shifted. The moment was not cinematic or triumphant. It felt sober. Measured. Heavy—the way truth often feels when it finally breaks through confusion. There was no applause. No swelling relief. Only a quiet, almost sacred steadiness—as if something chaotic had been forced to stand down.

The excerpt you just read captures that tension—the collision of relief and dread. Closure rarely feels the way we imagine it will. Sometimes it steadies us. Sometimes it exposes how deep the wound truly runs. Sometimes it compels us to confront the full weight of what happened.

But it does something essential: it anchors grief to reality instead of speculation.

And that matters more than we realize.

Unanswered questions can haunt more deeply than loss itself. The enemy thrives in unanswered questions. He magnifies them, stretches them, turns them into accusations.

Was it random? Was it preventable? Was God absent? Was I at fault?

The DNA evidence did not heal the grief. But it gave grief a boundary. It answered the question of who. It silenced the endless spiral of *what if*. It replaced suspicion with fact.

And facts stabilize.

In Scripture, truth is described as liberating:

> "And you will know the truth, and the truth will set you free."
>
> John 8:32 (ESV)

We often interpret that verse in purely spiritual terms—and rightly so. But truth also dismantles the enemy's primary weapon: deception. When truth enters a space clouded by uncertainty, it reduces chaos. It narrows the battlefield. It prevents lies from multiplying unchecked.

Closure is not the same as peace. But it creates the conditions in which peace can begin to take root.

There is something else I learned in that season: justice and vengeance are not the same thing.

When someone you love is taken violently, the desire for justice is natural. Beneath it, however, something darker can begin to stir—the desire not merely for accountability, but for retaliation. For suffering to be returned in equal measure. For pain to be mirrored back.

That instinct feels righteous. It feels powerful.

But it is not ours to carry.

Romans 12:19 is not poetic comfort; it is instruction:

> "Beloved, never avenge yourselves, but leave it to the wrath of God, for it is written, Vengeance is mine, I will repay, says the Lord."
>
> Romans 12:19 (ESV)

When the evidence confirmed the killer's identity, something holy happened beneath the surface. The burden shifted. Responsibility moved out of trembling human hands and into the hands of the justice system—and ultimately, into the hands of God.

That shift matters.

Because unresolved grief is fertile ground for bitterness. And bitterness is a foothold. It begins as pain but hardens into resentment. It persuades us to carry what God has already claimed as His responsibility.

In *La Llorona*, Mi-Ra struggles even after the evidence is found. That is intentional. Catching a killer does not silence memory. It does not undo trauma. It does not quiet a house at night.

But it removes ambiguity.

And ambiguity feeds fear.

One of the enemy's most consistent tactics is confusion—blurring lines, distorting motives, amplifying uncertainty until truth itself feels unstable. Confusion exhausts. Confusion isolates. Confusion whispers that nothing will ever be made right.

In this case, truth cut through that fog. Not to erase sorrow. Not to minimize loss. But to anchor it.

Healing rarely arrives as a single, dramatic breakthrough. It unfolds in layers: shock, anger, accusation, questions, answers—then the long, deliberate work of refusing to let grief become identity.

The DNA match was not resurrection.

But it was mercy.

It was light entering a space where deception could have taken root. It was evidence that justice, though delayed, was not absent. It was proof that even in devastation, God is attentive to detail.

Even a strand of dog hair matters.

Even the smallest fragment of truth can dismantle a stronghold of confusion.

And sometimes, God uses the most ordinary evidence to remind us that He has not surrendered the battlefield.

Chapter 13

The Burdened

A t its heart, *La Llorona: The Awakening* was born from raw encounters with grief—both personal and borrowed. It carries not only my own experiences with loss, but also the stories entrusted to me by others who allowed me to witness their sorrow up close.

Grief is universal. It levels us. It does not discriminate by age, beauty, strength, or faith. And because it is so deeply human, we often assume it is a battle we should be able to manage.

When we think about grief, the battlefield seems less ominous than spiritual warfare. It feels psychological. Emotional. Contained within the boundaries of human control. And if it is within our control, then surely we must be responsible for how we fight it.

If we collapse, we blame ourselves.

If we cannot move forward, we blame ourselves.

If someone else succumbs to despair, we search for what we missed.

Grief begins to feel like something we should master.

But that assumption is dangerous.

Because grief is not merely an emotion. It is a force. And when it mingles with regret, guilt, or unanswered questions, it becomes disorienting. It reshapes memory. It distorts perspective. It tempts us to carry burdens that were never ours to hold.

I learned this long before I had language for it.

Growing up, I often rode along as my parents delivered flower arrangements to cemeteries. Our flower shop stood across from the largest cemetery in San Antonio. Death was not abstract to me. It was logistical. Seasonal. Scheduled.

I saw rows of fresh graves before the grass had settled. I watched families dressed in black cling to one another beside open earth. I saw mothers collapse into sons, husbands standing rigid beside caskets, children staring in confusion as caskets were lowered into ground that would never return what it received.

But what marked me most were the letters.

The cards tucked into bouquets. The handwritten notes pressed beneath stones. Birthday balloons tied to metal stands. Plastic-wrapped pages weighed down so they would not blow away.

Grief, I learned, keeps speaking long after the funeral ends.

An Excerpt from *La Llorona: The Awakening*

The news sat heavy on Paul's tongue, metallic, unspoken, but inevitable. He stood in the doorway, every muscle strung taut, every breath like glass in his chest. Evelyn looked up from the couch, eyes wide, expectant, clinging to hope.

Paul's gaze faltered, the sadness in him too plain to hide. His eyes clouded with grief, giving him away before he could speak.

"Well, where is he?" Evelyn's voice sharpened, nervous laughter edging her words. "Why are you looking at me like that?"

Beside her, Evelyn's mother rose slowly, her face already pale with under-standing. "Let me take Delilah to the other room," she whispered. Gently, she lifted the baby from Evelyn's arms, holding her close as she slipped quietly down the hall.

Paul drew in a shuddering breath, the weight of the moment crushing down. His voice broke as he forced the words out. "He's gone, Evelyn. I'm so sorry. I didn't find him in time."

The words tasted like failure. He had delivered them as gently as he could, but there was no soft edge to tragedy. No way to dress it in anything but its brutal truth.

Evelyn's scream ripped through the house—raw, jagged—the kind of sound that made walls shudder and hearts seize. It wasn't just grief; it was rupture, the body splitting under a weight it was never built to bear. A sound Paul knew he would carry long after the house fell silent

But grief has a way of rearranging people. Evelyn was young, striking, composed. Easy for others to believe she would recover in time.

Paul knew better.

He was reminded of it every time he visited his brother's grave.

Evelyn's handwriting lived there—looped and unmistakable—scattered across greeting cards tucked carefully against the headstone. Their white corners peeked out from beneath wilting flowers, paper softening with damp and time. Offerings meant for James alone.

He told himself not to read them. That whatever Evelyn had written was private—between wife and husband. Sacred. Untouchable.

And still, his hands betrayed him.

One by one, he slid the cards free from their envelopes. The paper whispered as it opened, a sound too loud in the quiet of the cemetery. His eyes moved faster than his conscience could stop them, devouring words never meant for him—confessions, apologies, fragments of a marriage still speaking after death:

I love you more every day.

Every day without you is a punishment.

I can't go on without you.

I should have seen it. I should have stopped it.

Your silence was screaming at me and I ignored it.

If love was enough, you'd still be here.

Reflection

Now I understand.

Grief speaks long after the funeral ends. And sometimes it keeps speaking because it does not know how to stop.

Grief often carries guilt in its pocket. Not always rational guilt—but imagined responsibility.

I should have noticed. I should have called. I should have stayed. If I had done one thing differently...

This is where grief begins to distort.

Grief longs for resolution. It wants explanation. It wants one more conversation. And when it cannot have those things, it looks for somewhere to rest.

This is where the battle shifts.

Not into spectacle. Not into shadows. But into narrative.

When loss is sudden or violent, the mind begins reconstructing events. It searches for missed signals. It reorders timelines. It assigns responsibility. The heart replays the moment, whispering, *If I had done something differently...*

Regret attaches itself to memory. Guilt attaches itself to love.

And if those attachments are not examined in the light of truth, they begin to warp perception.

Left untethered, grief can shift from sorrow to self-accusation. From mourning to self-punishment. From heartbreak to harmful narrative. When it spirals unchecked, it does more than ache—it can consume.

I have seen it.

I have watched grief turn inward and become self-punishment. I have seen it convince someone they were responsible for what they could not control. I have watched sorrow harden into despair, and despair whisper that escape is easier than endurance.

Grief, when severed from hope, becomes dangerous.

It narrows vision. It magnifies regret. It isolates. It persuades the suffering person that their pain is permanent and their presence is a burden. And once a person begins agreeing with those lies, the spiral tightens.

When grief convinces us that we could have prevented what happened, it places an unbearable weight on the living. It assigns us omniscience we never possessed. It confuses sorrow with culpability.

This is where spiritual warfare often hides—not in dramatic manifestations, but in internal agreement with punishing thoughts:

You failed. You missed the signs. You weren't enough. If you had loved better, this wouldn't have happened.

These thoughts feel like accountability.

But often, they are accusation.

Scripture tells us that Satan is called "the accuser":

> "Now the salvation and the power and the kingdom of our God and the authority of his Christ have come, for the accuser of our brothers has been thrown down, who accuses them day and night before our God."
>
> Revelation 12:10 (ESV)

Notice the distinction: conviction leads to repentance and restoration. Accusation leads to shame and paralysis.

Evelyn's letters are heartbreaking not because she loved deeply, but because she assumes responsibility for what she could not control. I saw that same tone in countless cemetery cards growing up—people bargaining with silence, confessing to headstones, apologizing to stone.

Grief is human. Guilt is human. But self-condemnation is not healing.

> "For godly grief produces a repentance that leads to salvation without regret, whereas worldly grief produces death."
>
> 2 Corinthians 7:10 (ESV)

We do not control life and death. We love. We try. We show up imperfectly. And sometimes tragedy still comes.

The danger is not grief itself. The danger is believing we were sovereign when we never were.

> "Come to me, all who labor and are heavy laden, and I will give you rest.

Take my yoke upon you, and learn from me, for I am gentle and
lowly in heart, and you will find rest for your souls.
For my yoke is easy, and my burden is light."

Matthew 11:28–30 (ESV)

There is only One who holds life and death in His hands. And we are not
Him.

PART V

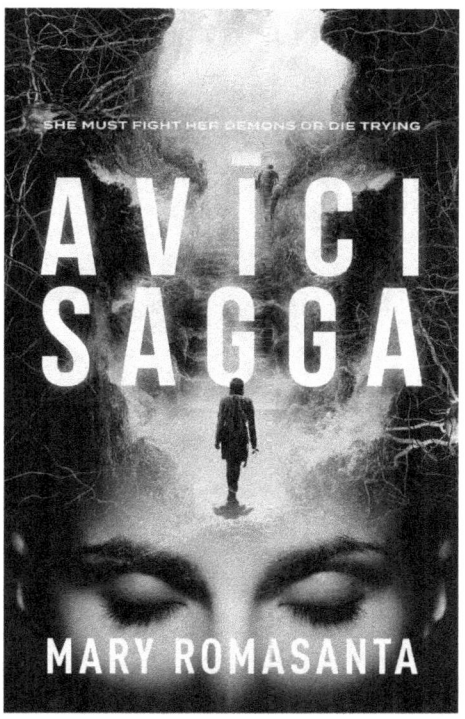

When recurring nightmares of a former love-interests begin to unravel 29-year-old Emma's health, she seeks help from a renowned psychiatrist and dream scientist. Together, they plunge into the labyrinth of her subconscious, confronting buried trauma and fractured truths. But as Emma's condition spirals, she discovers the stakes are far greater than sleepless nights. To survive, she must face her demons head-on—before they claim her life.

Chapter 14

The Cursed

The title of my debut novel, *Avīci Sagga*, is more than a distinctive name—it is a theological statement. It reflects the spiritual and emotional dualities at the core of the story.

In Buddhist tradition, Avīci is the lowest level of hell—a place of unrelenting torment reserved for the gravest transgressions. In Hindu belief, it is one of the hells governed by Yama, the god of death and justice, where souls endure the consequences of accumulated karma. In stark contrast, Sagga represents heaven—a realm of light, serenity, and divine reward.

Placed side by side, Avīci and Sagga form a spectrum. Not merely between damnation and paradise, but between despair and redemption, corruption and restoration, shadow and light.

My novel lives in that tension.

The characters wrestle with moral ambiguity, spiritual warfare, and questions that resist clean resolution. Every moment of dread is countered by a flicker of hope. Every fall is shadowed by the possibility of rising.

Avīci Sagga is about the battleground of the soul.

It explores what happens when the line between good and evil is not merely external—but internal. When temptation does not arrive as obvious darkness, but as something persuasive. Reasonable. Even compassionate.

What happened in *Infestation* was personal—rooted in a house, a place, a history. But what inspired *Avīci Sagga* cut deeper. It reached into the marrow of my faith and asked a far more unsettling question:

What if the most dangerous damage does not come from outside—but from within?

I once knew a woman whose story never made headlines. Her pain did not shout; it whispered. One day, someone showed me a stack of old photographs that had been found discarded in the street. Each photo was of her.

And in every single one, her eyes had been violently scratched out.

Not once.

Over and over.

What happened to that woman was not random.

It was warfare.

There was no note. No identified culprit. No tidy resolution. But there was a message—and spiritually, it was unmistakable.

This was not merely vandalism.

It was a declaration.

A deliberate assault on identity. On vision. On witness.

The eyes are often called the windows to the soul. To deface them is to attempt erasure—to silence someone's testimony, to obscure their discernment, to symbolically extinguish whatever light lives within them.

That act was not about paper and ink. It was about presence.

Avīci Sagga steps into those shadows—not only the ones that inhabit haunted spaces, but the ones that settle quietly in the human heart. It confronts the ways evil disguises itself as good intention. The bargains struck in desperation. The generational patterns handed down like heirlooms—heavy, inherited, and rarely questioned.

It is a story of survival.

Of reckoning.

Of reclaiming what darkness once tried to erase.

The excerpt that follows is more than narrative. It enters the tension between torment and redemption. It exposes the subtle negotiations of the soul—and asks what it truly costs to choose light when darkness feels justified.

An Excerpt from *Avīci Sagga*

EMMANUEL WOULD COME TO MAKE many mistakes throughout his life. He was not perfect; he never claimed to be. He lived, and learned, and owned up to his mistakes. But there was one mistake that haunted him, followed him, taunted him. It was a mistake that came with an insidious consequence. He gazed at Emma from across the table; his eyes filled with a haunting sadness.

"One night, after leaving the cantina, I came home to an empty house. I searched every room. I even looked under the bed. I thought your mother was playing games. Then it occurred to me to check her drawers. All her clothes were gone. She had left me.

"It mortified me, I did not know where she could be. Night after night, I searched for her aimlessly. I thought I had lost her forever. Not knowing what else to do, I went to see your abuela. I told her what happened, and she gave me a glimpse of hope."

"What did abuela say?"

"She told me about a curandera."

Brianna raised her hand. "What's a curandera?" she asked.

"It's pronounced coo-rrran-de-rrra." His tongue flicked back and forth as he effortlessly rolled the r's in the word. "It means woman healer. Many people in my culture believe that illness is linked with evil spirits and thus seek remedies from curanderas, who use simple herbs and holy water to cure physical, psychological, and even spiritual ailments.

"I had dark and sunken bags under my eyes and my mother said I had been cursed. She said it explained my dramatic change in looks and horrible behavior. She gave me the address of a curandera that she said could break the curse.

"That night, I sought the home of the curandera. Along the way, I came across an old tiendita, a little corner store. The tiendita's rusty tin roof and blue wooden siding gave it a sort of authentic Mexican charm that drew me to it. In my drunken stupor, I abandoned looking for the address my mother gave me and stumbled up the cement steps that led to the tiendita's porch. Its rusty screen door was closed but not locked, and the door behind it was wide open. Through the screen door, I saw an old woman sweeping the floors. She looked at me as if she had been expecting me. 'Are you the curandera?' I asked.

"'Yes,' she replied. Her hair was long and unkempt, mostly white, peppered with a few strands of black. She wore a long, tattered dress. It was crimson red, like the color of old blood.

"I pulled the screen door open to let myself in. Candles flickered over the windowsills.

"'What brings you here?' she asked.

"I fell to my knees and told her I wanted my wife back. 'I would give anything for a second chance with her,' I pleaded.

"She wiped a tear from my face. Her fingers were rough like sandpaper and as cold as ice. She put her finger in her mouth, as if savoring my tears. 'I want to help you, but I can't get rid of a curse that easily,' she said. 'The curse needs a new home.'

"'What do you mean?' I asked.

"'Your wife will bear a daughter,' she replied. 'This unborn child must carry the burden of your sins if you want a chance with your wife.'

"Like a fool, I accepted her terms."

An eerie silence cloaked the room. Emma and Brianna exchanged looks.

He continued, "I thought the curandera's words couldn't possibly come to fruition. And yet they haunted me, so I returned with my mother the next night. Surely there was something she could do, I thought. We pulled up to the tiendita.

"'What are we doing?' my mother asked.

"'This is the place,' I replied.

"I'll never forget the deep stare my mother gave me. 'No, it isn't,' she said.

"I hung my head down. I failed again.

"'There is nothing we can do now. Let's go inside,' she said.

"The building didn't have the same charm it had the previous night. The tiendita was cloaked in darkness. Weeds had taken over the front porch through its cracks. Its screen door was nailed shut. My mother ordered me to break it down.

"'You broke down the door?' Emma asked.

"I didn't need to. The frame around the door was rotted. With just one pull, the screen door opened. The door let out a high-pitched squeak that seemed to drag on forever as I pushed it open. The smell of mold and mildew filled our nostrils when we stepped in. The room was pitch black except for a small beam of light that shone through a crack in the boarded windows in the back. I lit a match.

"A shiver ran down my spine. It looked nothing like it did the night before. Overgrown weeds covered in thorns crept in from the backyard through more cracks in the boarded windows, giving it an eerie, haunted appearance. I looked up; the roof was sagging, the ceiling crumbling. It was a shell of what I remembered. I looked down; the floor was covered in dust, rat droppings, and cobwebs—evidence that the building had long been abandoned. I could not believe my eyes. 'I saw her sweeping, she was sweeping the whole time,' I told my mother.

"I noticed my mother kneeling on the floor. She was holding something. 'What is it?' I asked.

"'Let's go,' she replied. 'Now.'"

"She rushed to the car so fast that I struggled to keep up. In the car, she revealed what she had found."

He paused.

"It was a wedding photo of me and your mother. There were X's scratched over my eyes and over your mother's womb. My mother told me that the woman I saw was no curandera. She was a bruja."

Emma let out an audible gasp; her eyes bulged with disbelief.

He turned to Brianna. "Bruja is Spanish for witch. Brujas pray to spirits and practice witchcraft and black magic known as brujería, or witchery. But not all brujas are bad. Some practice white magic, a type of magic used for good or selfless purposes," he explained.

"Where did she get the photo?" Brianna asked. She appeared captivated by his story.

"I can only assume that I brought it to her, but I was drunk, and I truly don't remember. I don't think it matters much.

"My mother and I said nothing to each other the entire way back to her home. When we arrived, she ripped the photo into tiny pieces and ordered me to bring her a tin can. I sifted through a garbage bin outside, searching for a tin can, and brought it to her. She put the pieces of photo in the tin can. Then she lit a match, tossed it in the can, and burned the photo to ashes."

Emma and Brianna sat silently, their mouths agape.

"When I got home that night, your mother was waiting in the dining room. I told her what happened. I never went back to look for the curandera. Instead, from that day forward, we put all our faith in God and committed to serving Him together for the rest of our lives."

Reflection

In Scripture, curses are not treated as superstition or metaphor. They are described as real and consequential. From the covenant blessings and curses outlined in Deuteronomy 28 to the prophetic warnings throughout the Old Testament, Scripture presents obedience and rebellion as having tangible outcomes.

At the same time, the Bible does not portray curses as mystical forces operating independently of God's sovereignty. They are either consequences of disobedience, the fruit of idolatry and injustice, or the result of alignment with spiritual rebellion. They are not arbitrary. They are relational.

Biblically, patterns of hardship—repeated cycles of strife, oppression, sickness, or destruction—are sometimes described as consequences that echo beyond a single moment of sin. Scripture acknowledges that the effects of rebellion can ripple outward, impacting families and generations (Exodus 20:5). But it also insists that each person is responsible for their own response before God (Ezekiel 18:20).

This tension matters.

We often imagine spiritual battles unfolding in dramatic settings—dark rituals, violent manifestations, overt confrontation. But more often, they slip quietly into ordinary life. They settle into homes, routines, relationships, and family histories. And if we are not discerning, they take root slowly—less like an explosion and more like erosion.

Stories like the one you've just read do not emerge from exaggeration. They rise from the intersection of truth and trauma. Evil rarely announces itself with spectacle. More often, it weaves itself into family systems, into inherited wounds, into habits formed for survival, into pain that was never acknowledged or healed.

The language of "curse" may sound archaic or uncomfortable to modern ears. But biblically, a curse represents alignment with something opposed to God's design. It is not magic. It is not myth. It is agreement—sometimes willful, sometimes inherited, sometimes unconscious—with patterns that produce bondage rather than freedom.

These patterns may express themselves as cycles of addiction, abuse, occult involvement, chronic fear, poverty, rejection, or despair—realities that seem to "run in the family." While psychology explains some of these cycles through trauma and learned behavior, spiritual warfare asks an additional question: Where has darkness found agreement?

Scripture is explicit about the nature of this conflict:

> "For we do not wrestle against flesh and blood, but against the rulers, against the authorities, against the cosmic powers over this present darkness, against the spiritual forces of evil in the heavenly places."
>
> Ephesians 6:12 (ESV)

Curses do not simply disappear on their own.

Left unaddressed, they linger—quietly, persistently—festering in silence and weaving themselves into families like invisible chains. For a long time, I believed that what "ran in the family" was just chance, temperament, or coincidence. A string of unfortunate similarities. But spiritual warfare teaches us otherwise. It reveals that patterns are rarely random.

Cycles of fear, addiction, shame, rejection, abuse, or despair often point to something deeper—a curse that has taken root. These patterns don't just repeat behavior; they shape identity. And while we may inherit the wound, we are not destined to inherit the bondage. In Christ, inheritance can be interrupted.

Breaking a curse begins with repentance—not only for our own sins, but for the sins of those who came before us. This is one of the hardest truths to accept. As a child, I struggled to understand why I should bear the spiritual weight of decisions I never made. But repentance is not about blame or punishment; it is about closure. It is about identifying where a door was opened and intentionally shutting it.

When we acknowledge sin—personal or generational—confess it before God, and ask for His forgiveness, we remove the legal foothold the enemy has used to operate across generations. Repentance strips darkness of its claim. It restores spiritual order where chaos once ruled.

Next comes renunciation. This step is active and deliberate. It is not enough to silently hope that a curse lifts on its own—we must confront it. With our own voices, we reject the lie, sever agreement with darkness, and declare that it no longer has authority in our lives. Words carry spiritual weight. Just as curses are spoken into existence, they must be broken aloud.

But the true foundation—the immovable center of it all—is our authority in Christ.

Scripture makes this unmistakably clear:

> "Christ redeemed us from the curse of the law by becoming a curse for us—for it is written, "Cursed is everyone who is hanged on a tree."
>
> Galatians 3:13 (ESV)

This truth is not symbolic. It is central.

What Jesus bore on the cross, I do not have to bear.

He did not merely sympathize with our suffering—He absorbed it. He did not simply acknowledge the curse—He became it, so that we would not have to live beneath its weight (Galatians 3:13). The cross was not metaphor. It was substitution.

The enemy thrives on convincing believers that they are trapped—that history is stronger than redemption, that the sins of the past outweigh the promise of the present. He whispers that cycles cannot be broken, that wounds define destiny, that freedom is theological language but not lived reality.

But in Christ, the cycle ends.

Not because pain disappears overnight. Not because consequences evaporate. But because the legal claim of the curse has been satisfied.

We are not powerless victims of generational patterns or spiritual inheritance gone wrong. We are sons and daughters—adopted, redeemed, restored—standing in freedom purchased with blood. Our authority does not originate in our strength, discipline, or insight. It rests in our union with Christ.

We carry authority not because of who we are, but because of whose we are.

And with that authority, we confront what no longer has permission to remain.

Then there is deliverance prayer.

Not a formula. Not an incantation. Not magic words spoken into the air.

Deliverance is not spectacle—it is surrender coupled with authority. It is a cry to God and a command to darkness. It is the believer standing in Christ's finished work and applying it where bondage still lingers.

In deliverance, what has influenced is confronted. What has oppressed is named. What has lingered in shadow is brought into light. Fear is displaced by peace. Shame gives way to dignity. Silence is replaced with testimony. Heaviness lifts as freedom takes root.

This is not theory to me.

This is lived experience.

I have prayed those prayers. I have watched doors close that once stood wide open to destruction—and new doors open where I believed there were only walls. I have felt shame lift in ways I cannot fully explain, except to say that what once felt permanent lost its grip. What once defined me no longer had authority to speak my name.

Curses may be real. Their effects may be felt. Their shadows may linger.
But they are not final.
Christ is.

Chapter 15

The Possessed

Early in his ministry, my father met a man who would permanently alter his spiritual course. This was not someone who merely spoke about spiritual warfare as a concept. He lived it. He carried an urgency that unsettled complacency and a conviction that refused to reduce the unseen to metaphor. With clarity and authority, he introduced my father to the biblical reality of demonic strongholds—and the mandate to confront them directly.

That encounter ignited something that has never faded.

From that point forward, my father devoted a significant portion of his ministry to deliverance—praying for the tormented, anointing homes, confronting demonic oppression, and standing in the gap for those who felt bound and voiceless. By his own count, he has led more than fifty exorcisms and assisted in many more.

The work was not glamorous. It was often misunderstood. At times, it was resisted. It was always spiritually demanding. But it was necessary.

With decades of pastoral experience and a calling marked by discernment, my father has seen what many prefer to ignore. He does not sensationalize the unseen—he confronts it. He has walked into rooms where the atmosphere shifted under invisible weight. He has prayed with those tormented by forces they could not name. He has laid hands on the possessed and watched clarity return where chaos once ruled.

Deliverance, for him, was never theory. It was obedience.

I grew up hearing fragments of those stories—whispers shared in careful tones, details revealed only when needed. Some of those memories blur with time. They drift at the edges of recollection.

But one memory remains sharp. One I witnessed with my own eyes. It does not drift quietly. It strikes like a storm—urgent, undeniable, unforgettable.

For years, I wrestled with whether to tell this story plainly. It would have been easier to bury it in metaphor—tucked safely inside fiction, softened by pacing, veiled by theme. For a time, I did exactly that. I scattered pieces of it into my novels, allowing characters to carry what I was not yet ready to name directly.

But as I have grown—in faith, in courage, and in calling—I have come to understand something unshakable:

Some stories must be told without disguise. Darkness does not retreat because we avoid naming it. Silence is not protection. It can become permission. When we refuse to speak about the battles we have witnessed—or the freedom we have seen—we do not shield others. We leave them unprepared.

This chapter is about demonic possession—but not the spectacle popular culture portrays. There are no theatrics here. No exaggerated horror. No sensationalism.

It is a story about discernment. About faith tested in intimate spaces. And about what it truly takes to confront darkness—and see freedom prevail.

An Excerpt from *Avīci Sagga*

EMMA STOOD NEXT TO HER father at the entrance of the church as the congregation trickled in for Sunday evening service when a visitor stepped up to enter the church. She came alone.

"Welcome, sister. Please, sit anywhere you'd like," Emma's father said, shaking the woman's hand.

"Thank you, Pastor," she replied.

Emma extended her hand to shake the woman's hand. Her father swiftly intercepted and picked her up. "Let's go inside, sweetheart. Service is about to begin."

The service began with worship and praise music, as it always did. Emma's father stepped up to the podium to begin the sermon. He opened his Bible to the book of Corinthians. "For the word of the cross is folly to those who are perishing, but to us who are being saved, it is the power of God," he read. He looked up at the congregation. "That's a powerful message."

His attention turned to a loud, sinister cackle coming from the back.

"Sister? Is something funny?" he asked.

It was the visitor. She laughed again, mouth closed, her smile all too wide.

"Do you need prayer?" he asked.

"No hablo inglés," the woman said in a deep and raspy voice, not the same voice she came in with.

"¿Cómo te llamas?" he asked.

"¡No, cabrón!" she growled. She spat as she spoke. Her mouth overflowed with saliva.

He pointed at her. "Come here, demon!" he demanded.

The woman cackled as she remained firmly planted in her seat.

He turned to a group of men sitting at the front of the church. "Bring her to me." He spoke in a commanding tone.

The men approached the woman and lifted her from her seat. The woman kicked and screamed intensely; her limbs contorted in ways Emma didn't know possible as she fought to escape.

"She's very strong," one of the men said, his voice quivering. She swung her head from right to left. Her teeth were clenched but visible, like a dog about to bite. Her fangs appeared to descend from her gums.

Emma's eyes widened in disbelief.

"¡Saca a los niños! Remove the children!" her father ordered.

Her mother grabbed her hand. "Let's go, now," she said.

"Mommy, what's happening? Where are we going?"

"We're going to the car," her mother replied. "We need to run."

"Why?"

She looked down at her. "Because you're too young to see this."

"I've never witnessed a full exorcism," Emma said. "Until now, I mean."

"Interesting." Dr. Clark said, folding his arms across his chest.

Emma sensed he wasn't convinced.

"I have witnessed a demonic possession, though," she said.

"What's the difference?" he asked.

"Someone can be possessed without having the demon exorcised. In my case, I witnessed a woman that was demonically possessed, but I didn't see the exorcism my father performed."

"I see," he replied. "Would you care to tell me more?"

She inhaled deeply.

"I was a child when it happened. I was rushed out of my father's church by my mother when it became clear that a woman visiting that night was demonically possessed. It wasn't until I was older that my father told me what unfolded inside."

She thought back to what her father told her had happened in the church that night while she waited in the car with her mother. She remembered how terrified she felt as it was happening. Over the years, though, she hadn't given it much thought.

"Are you comfortable telling me about it?" he asked.

She nodded. Since experiencing what happened with Davis firsthand, the thought of what happened that night didn't scare her nearly as much as it used to.

"It took four men to hold her down. My father saw fear in one of the men's eyes and told him to wait outside. The man pleaded with him. He wanted to stay and help, but my father said he wasn't ready to be there and called upon a co-pastor to take his place. He ordered everyone else to join hands and pray from outside. When everyone was out of the church, my father asked for the demon's name. She lunged at him. The men struggled to hold her back. The demon cackled in delight. It said its name was Juan; it spoke in a deep and ominous voice, but not a clear one."

"What do you mean?"

"My father told me the voice was muffled, garbled, choppy, even high-pitched. He said it was as though the voice was coming through a broken speaker being filtered through layers of interference. He ordered the demon to leave the woman and rubbed his hands with anointed oil. The demon began growling obscenities at my father. It was as though it knew what my father intended to do next."

"What did he intend to do?"

"He was going to form a cross on the woman's forehead using the anointed oil. Her head turned from right to left as she resisted. The demon screeched in agony as the oil contacted the woman's forehead. It snarled and growled. She showed her teeth, signaling she was ready to bite. They pulled the woman's legs from under her, and each held her down by a limb. Then he placed the Bible on her stomach.

"The woman screamed in agony when the Bible touched her body, as if she had just been branded. She pleaded with my father to remove it. As she pleaded, my father told me she spoke in the woman's voice, not the demon's voice, and that she had a look of sincerity in her eyes. The men asked my father if they should release her. My father said the demon was trying to fool them. He knelt and placed his hand on the visitor's forehead and commanded the demon out. The woman's back arched and her body jerked, then she convulsed and foamed at the mouth. After some time, the woman lay motionless on the floor, sleeping peacefully. The demon was gone."

Reflection

What I witnessed that night as a child—before I was hurried out of the church—became a turning point for me. Until then, I had only heard the stories of spiritual warfare. I had read about miracles, deliverance, and demonic oppression.

But that night, I saw it with my own eyes. I heard a demon speak through a human voice. I saw its incisors pushed unnaturally from the gums. I heard it hiss. I saw it thrash, kick, and scream as it was dragged toward the altar. I watched it resist the name of Jesus. That moment became a cornerstone in my understanding of faith—not as comfort, but as combat; not as tradition, but as authority.

That was the night I stopped questioning whether demons and darkness were real—and began living with the conviction that light was not only just as real, but far more powerful.

I believe my father understood what he was allowing into the church that night. Another congregation might have turned the visitor away at the door. Another might never have discerned what was coming. The event lies so far in the past now that my father, well into his eighties, has lost some of the details. But whatever the reason—his instinct, his conviction, or simply his obedience—he allowed the visitor to enter.

My father always told me, "The world is full of spirits—some holy, some not. And you must be spiritually ready, like a soldier trained for war." I didn't fully grasp the weight of his words until I had lived through moments that shattered the veil between the seen and unseen. Moments that didn't just frighten me—they transformed me. Because in them, I saw the power of God on full display. I saw what it means to call on the name of Jesus and watch darkness tremble.

What happened that night wasn't theater. It wasn't folklore, superstition, or fear-mongering. It wasn't the stuff of movies or ghost stories. It was a spiritual confrontation not between people, but between realms—a moment that made it clear: evil is not an abstract concept. It's active. Intentional. Strategic.

But it was also defeated.

That's what we must remember. Evil exists. But it doesn't endure. It cannot win—not when it's up against the name, the blood, and the authority of Christ. Darkness thrives in silence, in confusion, in isolation. It gains ground when we're too afraid to speak, too unsure to stand, too distracted to pray. But when we shine the light of truth—real truth—it loses its grip. And this is why I tell my story. Not for shock. Not for spectacle. But for freedom.

Scripture tells us:

> "And they have conquered him by the blood of the Lamb and by the word of their testimony, for they loved not their lives even unto death."
>
> Revelation 12:11 (ESV)

That verse is not just encouragement—it's a battle strategy. The blood of Jesus breaks the curse. Our testimony breaks the silence. Together, they break the chains.

Chapter 16

The Delivered

It would be many years before I fully understood—let alone knew how to steward—the lessons and experiences of my past. As a child, and even well into adulthood, much of it felt exaggerated, almost unreal. Like stories meant to frighten rather than to form.

At times, I dismissed what I had lived through as emotional imprinting—a scare tactic dressed up as spiritual warning. Something easier to file away as imagination than to confront as truth. To accept it as real would have required admitting that the world was more layered—and more perilous—than I was prepared to acknowledge.

It was safer to minimize it.

To reckon with those experiences demanded a maturity I did not yet possess and a courage I had not yet cultivated. It required me to see my past not as coincidence or overreaction, but as preparation. So I rationalized it. I told myself those moments belonged to a version of faith that was too intense, too dramatic, too inconvenient to integrate into a life shaped by logic and control.

But truth has a way of waiting.

It does not demand attention. It does not force itself into view. It waits—quietly, patiently—until you are ready to face it not as fear, but as revelation. Until you recognize that what once unsettled you was not meant to haunt you, but to equip you.

The excerpt that follows is not allegory. It is confrontation.

It is the collision of truth and deception—light pressing against encroaching darkness. It is not a struggle of flesh and blood, not something that can be dismissed with reason or resolved by logic alone. It is a battle Scripture names plainly: powers and principalities, forces unseen yet undeniably felt in the deepest places of the soul.

This is the war the Bible speaks of.

This is the battle many endure in silence.

And this is the place where deliverance ceases to be theory or theological debate and becomes necessity.

An Excerpt from *Avīci Sagga*

As Emma looked on, stunned, a Bible scripture she memorized as a child flashed across her mind as if being broadcasted by an emergency alert system.

He said to them, 'Go!' So they came out and went into the pigs, and the whole herd rushed down the steep bank into the lake and died in the water.

Dr. Clark returned to the observation area. "It's locked. Now what do we do?" he asked, hands still trembling.

It was clear to her now. "The demons will need something to attach to when they leave Davis's body. They need a new host."

"We can use the lab rats," Dr. Clark replied.

They exchanged nods.

Dr. Clark sprinted out of the sleep laboratory.

Emma followed the light that shone from his phone to navigate through the dark, hollow halls of the building.

They entered a research lab.

"Let's get them in a single cage," she said. She pulled a cage from the shelf and placed it on the floor.

Dr. Clark opened the cages; one by one, he passed the rats to Emma. "That's all of them. Let's go," he said, lifting the rat-filled cage.

The echo of malevolent voices boomed through the halls as they ran out of the research lab.

Leave!

¡Vete!

¡Vete!

Leave!

¡Vete!

¡Vete!

"Leave!" the voices shouted with a thunderous sound.

They entered the sleep laboratory and sprinted back to the observation area.

Emma looked at the video monitor. "He's foaming at the mouth. I need to get in there before it's too late."

He handed her the key.

"Before I go, I need you to repeat after me, 'I plead the blood of Jesus,'" she said.

"I plead the blood of Jesus?"

She nodded. "I need you to keep repeating that. The words act like a shield. The demons won't attack you if you're pleading the blood of Christ. Do you understand?"

He nodded. "I plead the blood of Jesus."

She turned, as she stepped toward the observation room, a feeling of tension consumed every muscle in her body. After a month of little food, sleep and mounting anxiety, her body was prepared to give up, whether she wanted it to or not. Her shoulders hunched forward; her body bent over.

"Emma!" Dr. Clark shouted. He stepped toward her.

"Stay there!" she ordered. "Just do what I told you and stay where you are, no matter what!"

She placed her hand over her stomach and winced, her face contorted with pain from the now life-threatening effects of stress on her body. Still, she persisted forward.

She looked through the observation window; a cloak of darkness blanketed the room, illuminated only by the smoldering embers of the demon's eyes. She yelled out in pain as she fought against her body's pleas to lie down.

Her quivering legs betrayed her will to keep going. She grunted and moaned as she fought to take just one more step.

Unable to move any farther, she planted her trembling hand on the frigid metal surface of the door and fell to her knees.

"It can't end like this...God help me," she whispered.

Her body jolted with an electrifying surge as she rested her forehead on the door, resuscitating her near lifeless body. Her head pulled back as she fell to the floor.

"Emma!" Dr. Clark shouted.

She lifted her head.

"Stay there and do as I said!" she shouted in a commanding voice.

She examined her hands and leg no longer quivering or in pain. With steady hands, she lifted herself from the floor, picked up the cage and inserted the key; a tremor of energy pulsed through her body.

The voices shouted with a thunderous sound:

Leave!

¡Vete!

¡Vete!

Leave!

The lights powered on as she opened the door. A deafening crash reverberated through the walls as the flying objects fell to the floor in unison the moment she stepped foot in.

"Emma, sweetheart, please... help me," the demon said.

She recognized the voice...

It was the voice of the man she fell in love with.

She looked into his hazel eyes, no longer a fiery red glow.

She smiled but was not fooled as she placed the cage on the floor by his bedside and looked at him with an unwavering gaze. "You no longer have any power over me, and you never will again," she said.

His eyes, no longer hazel, blazed with a fiery intensity as he growled demonically; his shoulders lunged forward like a rabid animal trying to attack.

She stepped out of the room and returned to the observation area, reaching for Dr. Clark's hand.

"We plead the blood of Jesus," they said together. Their breaths formed a cloud of fog with every exhale.

She looked at the video monitor. He was foaming at the mouth.

"Should we do something?" Dr. Clark asked.

"Keep pleading!" she shouted.

He nodded.

She got on her knees and bowed her head.

Dr. Clark knelt beside her.

"We plead the blood of Jesus," they continued.

A gentle stillness settled upon the room. She lifted her head and turned to the video monitor. They watched as Davis's body fell to the bed as though released from the grip of evil forces.

She opened her mouth lightly and exhaled.

The fog was gone.

Dr. Clark turned to her. "Does this mean it's over?"

Reflection

For a long time, I believed my past was something to survive rather than something to steward. The memories felt excessive inconvenient—too heavy to carry into adulthood without questioning their validity. So I did what many do: I compartmentalized. I explained away what unsettled me. I softened what demanded attention. I told myself those experiences belonged to a faith that was overly intense, better left behind in childhood where imagination could safely shoulder the blame.

That choice made life simpler. It also made me unprepared.

What I didn't understand then—but see clearly now—is that God wastes nothing. Not fear. Not trauma. Not even the moments that once felt unbearable. What I dismissed as exaggeration was preparation. What I labeled as scare tactics were warnings. What I tried to forget were tools meant for a future battle I hadn't yet stepped into.

Truth waited for me.

It didn't rush me or force itself into my understanding. It waited until I had the maturity to recognize it not as terror, but as training. Until I could see that those early encounters were not meant to paralyze me, but to teach me discernment. Not to haunt me, but to equip me. Not to glorify darkness, but to reveal the power of light when it is wielded with authority and faith.

That is why the excerpt from *Avīci Sagga* matters here.

Emma's confrontation is not fiction born from imagination—it is theology lived out in narrative form. It mirrors what Scripture has always taught: that demons seek hosts, that authority matters, that the name and blood of Jesus are not symbolic protections but active defenses. What unfolds in that laboratory is not sensationalism; it is a dramatized truth of spiritual warfare—the kind that drains the body, tests the will, and forces a decision between fear and faith.

Emma does not win because she is strong. She wins because she remembers who holds authority. Scripture tells us:

> "Put on the whole armor of God, that you may be able to stand against the schemes of the devil. For we do not wrestle against flesh and blood, but against the rulers, against the authorities, against the cosmic powers over this present darkness, against the spiritual forces of evil in the heavenly places. Therefore take up the whole armor of God, that you may be able to withstand in the evil day, and having done all, to stand firm."
>
> Ephesians 6:11-13 (ESV)

She pleads the blood of Jesus not as ritual, but as reality. She stands not because she feels capable, but because she understands that deliverance is never about human endurance—it is about divine intervention meeting obedience. Even when her body collapses, her spirit rises. Even when the enemy mimics love, familiarity, and intimacy, she is no longer fooled.

And that is the point.

Deliverance is rarely clean or dramatic in the way we expect. It is costly. It requires clarity under pressure and obedience when the body begs to retreat. It demands that we recognize deception even when it wears the voice of someone we love.

When Dr. Clark asks, "Does this mean it's over?" he is voicing the question we all ask after confrontation with darkness. The answer, as Scripture teaches us, is layered. One battle may end—but the war continues. Not because victory is uncertain, but because vigilance is required.

This chapter ends here not to resolve everything neatly, but to leave us with a sober truth: spiritual warfare is not theoretical, deliverance is not optional, and authority is not automatic unless it is exercised.

What once felt exaggerated now feels essential. What once felt unreal now feels urgent.

And what I once tried to forget has become the very lens through which I now understand freedom.

Because deliverance is not about escaping darkness forever. It is about learning how to stand when it comes.

Chapter 17

Conclusion

Deliverance is not passive. It demands preparation. It demands awareness. And often, it demands confrontation. Some battles begin before our feet ever touch the floor in the morning—before our minds are fully awake, before our hearts have found their rhythm for the day.

Why?

Because the enemy does not wait for us to rise. He does not announce himself. He moves in shadows, sowing fear while we sleep, whispering lies into the vulnerable space between dreams and waking. He seeks to disorient us before we can anchor ourselves in truth, to weaken us before we remember who we are and whose we are.

But here is the truth that changes everything: victory is not determined by when the battle begins. It is determined by who steps into the fight. And victory does not rest on our strength, our resolve, or our endurance—it rests on His presence.

Deliverance requires courage. The courage to speak truth when silence would feel safer. The courage to name what is broken instead of pretending it is whole. The courage to resist what is false, even when the lie has become familiar and comfortable.

It is the courage to bear the crushing weight of honesty—honesty about pain, about fear, about spiritual opposition—even when that honesty feels unbearable.

Deliverance is the decision to fight back. Not because the battle is easy, but because surrender is not an option. It is standing firm in the face of darkness, not with bravado, but with confidence rooted in the knowledge that darkness cannot claim what belongs to God. It is remembering, even when everything around us feels unstable, that we have never been abandoned. Not then. Not now. Not ever.

And yet, too often, we reduce spiritual warfare to metaphor. We relegate it to the past, treat it as an outdated belief, or allow it to exist only as spectacle—sensationalized on movie screens and dismissed in real life.

But spiritual warfare is no symbol. It is not an ancient idea buried in Scripture and irrelevant to modern life. It is not imagination or exaggeration or psychological projection. It is real. And just as real is spiritual victory.

So, should We Fight *for* Deliverance?

No.

We should fight *from* deliverance.

That distinction matters more than we often realize. Fighting *for* deliverance implies that freedom is still out of reach—that we are trapped, powerless, striving to earn what has not yet been granted. It places the burden on human effort, as though victory depends on endurance, discipline, or spiritual performance.

But fighting *from* deliverance tells a different story. It means you are already standing on ground Christ secured. It means the chains have already been broken, the authority has already been given, and the outcome has already been decided. You are not battling toward freedom—you are defending freedom that has been purchased at great cost.

Deliverance is not something you chase. It is the inheritance you step into. When you fight from deliverance, you fight with confidence—not arrogance, but assurance. You fight knowing that the enemy is not equal to you, because he is not equal to Christ. You fight knowing that what once held you no longer has permission to remain.

Deliverance is more than rescue. More than escape. More than relief. Deliverance is revelation.

It is the unveiling of what was hidden—the exposure of lies we did not know we had agreed with. It is the uncovering of deception, the breaking of chains that were never meant to bind us in the first place. It is light flooding dark corners where the enemy quietly took residence, the tearing down of strongholds he carefully constructed, and the reclaiming of territory he arrogantly assumed belonged to him.

The delivered do not cower. The delivered do not live in fear. The delivered stand tall—covered by the blood of Christ, called by His name, and claimed as His own.

Scripture affirms this unmistakably:

> "If the Spirit of him who raised Jesus from the dead dwells in you, he who raised Christ Jesus from the dead will also give life to your mortal bodies through his Spirit who dwells in you."
>
> Romans 8:11 (ESV)

Where the Spirit of God dwells, death cannot rule. Where Christ reigns, darkness cannot remain.

So stand firm. Speak truth. Walk in the authority you have been given.

> "Little children, you are from God and have overcome them, for he who is in you is greater than he who is in the world."
>
> 1 John 4:4 (ESV)

The battle may rage. It may feel relentless. It may feel overwhelming at times. But make no mistake—the outcome is not in question.

We are not fighting for a victory that might come. We are standing in a victory that already has. The war is not over. But the victory belongs to Christ. And in Him, it belongs to us.

Afterword

Since becoming an author, I have never hidden my motivation for writing: darkness exists. Not metaphorical darkness. Not poetic shadows. *Real darkness.* The kind that hides in silence. The kind that fractures families and wounds children. The kind that whispers lies into weak spirits and vulnerable hearts.

Through my stories, I don't aim to sensationalize it—or dismiss it as less threatening than it is. My mission is far simpler, and far more urgent: *to expose it.* To call it what it is. To drag it into the light. Because stories have power—not just to entertain, but to reveal, to awaken, and to confront what most would rather keep hidden.

At the start of this book, I recalled a television interview with the Archdiocese of San Antonio. The reporter leaned in and asked: "Given your upbringing in the Church—and living across from a cemetery—did you have a lot of nightmares growing up?" Recall, I answered, "All the time."

Then came the second question, one that lingered in the air far longer: "Do you *still* have nightmares?" This time, my answer came slower, more deliberate: "On occasion... but not like before."

I still dream vividly. And yes, sometimes the shadows try to creep back in. But now I meet them with discernment. Because I am no longer the frightened little girl clinging to her blanket, praying that something—or Someone—might protect her. I know now that Someone always did. But more importantly, I now understand who lives in me.

With time came growth—not just in age, but in *spiritual authority.* My faith deepened. My discernment sharpened. And when spiritual attacks became clearer, more frequent, I began to recognize them for what they were. Even in dreams, I began to change. I learned to stand. To speak. To pray with power.

Even asleep, I now fight back. And there is power in that—knowing you don't have to wake up to start winning. You can reclaim your mind in the middle of the night. There is something profoundly redemptive about reclaiming the ground you once feared to stand on. About going back to the very place you once trembled and saying: "*Not today.*"

What once haunted me now reminds me that I am not alone. I don't wake up afraid anymore. I wake up anchored in faith. I wake up armed with a spiritual badge and a mantle of authority. Because now, when the dark shows up—I show up too. I don't tremble anymore. I don't let nightmares write my story. I speak truth. I carry light. And I walk in the Name that makes darkness flee.

Acknowledgements

This book would not exist without the unwavering support, guidance, and love of so many people:

First and foremost, to my husband, Robert—my best friend, greatest champion, and steadfast partner in every chapter of life (and in every draft of this manuscript). Thank you for believing in me, for late-night brainstorming sessions, and for holding our three boys so I could chase down memories in dusty archives and quiet corners of my mind. And to our sons, whose laughter brightens even the darkest stories: you inspire me to keep writing, to keep believing in the power of hope and deliverance.

To my father, whose decades of ministry, deliverance work, and deep theological insight laid the foundation for this book. Your stories, wisdom, and example have shaped not only my faith but every page of *Deliver Us*.

To my mother, whose flower shop across from the cemetery gave me my first lessons in the mysteries that lie just beyond our sight—and whose quiet strength reminds me that beauty can flourish even amid decay.

To my brother, who not only witnessed some of these things with me, but helped me carry them. Your courage, faith, and big-brother steadiness anchored me through those years and through the writing of this book. Thank you for walking beside me through it all.

Finally, to the readers: thank you for opening your hearts to stories of darkness and redemption. May this book encourage you to confront what lurks unseen, to seek deliverance where it is needed most, and to believe in the transformative power of grace.

More from the Author

MARY ROMASANTA

In this powerful reimagining of the La Llorona legend, Mary Romasanta weaves together a chilling thriller and a poignant narrative of human connection, daring readers to confront the darkest depths of grief and find hope waiting on the other side.

After losing her husband and two children, Ma-Ri faces devastating tragedy. Wracked with grief and guilt, she succumbs to the siren call of despair, haunted by the ghostly legend of La Llorona—the Weeping Woman said to lure the grieving to their doom. But her daughter-in-law, Ruth, a determined technologist driven by love and loss, isn't ready to let her go.

About the Author

Mary Romasanta, an author, technologist, and mother of three young boys, embarked on a journey to transform her lifelong passion for writing into a reality after twenty years in her corporate career. Pushing past the boundaries of conventional genres, she delves into a unique blend of psychological thriller, science fiction, horror, and spirituality.

Raised in the heart of San Antonio, Texas, mere steps away from the sprawling expanse of the city's largest cemetery, Romasanta grew up surrounded by the mystique of the supernatural. The daughter of a pastor and florist, she drew inspiration from her childhood fascinations with the ethereal and spirituality to paint the vivid backdrops of her novels.

With her unique blend of genres and her unwavering dedication to cultural understanding weaved into her storytelling, Romasanta invites her readers to explore the depths of the human psyche, question the fabric of reality, and confront the terror lurking in the shadows.

FOR A COMPLETE LIST OF BOOKS BY

MARY ROMASANTA

VISIT

MaryRomasanta.com

Follow Mary Romasanta on Instagram

@AuthorMaryRomasanta